101 Handy Tech Tips for the iPhone

101 Handy Tech Tips for the iPhone

updated, Simplified and Revised for iOS 12

Rich DeMuro

For Mom, who taught me to believe in myself.

For Dad, who taught me the value of hard work.

For Lyndsey, who taught me that everything is possible.

For Parker and Tanner, who taught me what really matters.

Contents

PART I.
WHAT'S NEW IN IOS 12

PART II.
THE ESSENTIALS

PART III.
PRIVACY AND SECURITY

PART IV.
FUN TRICKS

PART V.
TAKE CONTROL

PART VI.
PHOTOS

PART VII.
SIRI

PART VIII.
TOOLS

PART IX.
MEDIA

PART X.
PRODUCTIVITY

PART XI.
WELLNESS

PART XII.
SURFING THE WEB

PART XIII.
BONUS TIP

Introduction

It was summer 2007 and I was ready for what Apple was about to unleash on the world. I was standing outside their retail store in New York City with what seemed like thousands of other people. We were all waiting for the launch of the iPhone. At the time, I was a reporter for the technology website CNET, and this would be one of the biggest stories of my fledgling career.

I was already obsessed with cell phones, but the iPhone was a totally new breed of machine. One that could make phone calls, surf the real internet and serve as a music player too. In short, it was nearly the perfect device for someone commuting their way into the city each day, like me. At that point, early buyers were familiar with a video of Steve Jobs introducing the device on stage at an Apple Event, but that's about all we had to go on. Outside the Apple store, there were giant screens in the shape of an iPhone playing a video loop of some prominent features – making calls, playing videos, surfing the web and listening to music all seemed magical on this new device.

It wasn't that these things weren't possible on other devices at the time. We were used to doing email on BlackBerry and my Motorola Q let me surf the web, but nothing prepared us for the iPhone. It revolutionized how we thought about our phones. Suddenly, we had entertainment, information and the ability to do real stuff on our phones. Of course, what we now think about the iPhone wasn't available back then. There was no App Store. No high-speed internet. No turn by turn navigation. All of those things would come in time, but the stage was set.

This was the device that would set the standard for mobile communications for years to come. It still does.

This book is all about getting the most out of your iPhone using the software that's already on there. The beauty of Apple's mobile operating system – iOS, as it's called – is that it does the basics pretty easily and intuitively. There is no instruction manual inside the box. But press a little harder, swipe in a different way or pull down on the screen, and you reveal functions you never knew were there.

You might already be aware of some of the tips and features I'm about to lead you through, and that's OK. My hope is that this book helps you discover one, two or twenty-five little things you didn't realize were possible with the device you're carrying daily.

Rich DeMuro

richontech.tv

How to use this book

The idea behind this book is that it contains the functionality I feel like every iPhone user should at least be aware of. It's not an instruction manual, nor a complete list of every feature the iPhone offers. It's a way to make you feel like you are getting the most out of your device, customize it to work for you and remove some of the little frustrations that go along with life in the digital age.

You can read it from cover to cover, search for a keyword or jump to a section you want to learn more about. My hope is that you read about a feature today so it's in your head for the future when you suddenly realize you need it.

The bigger point is to build awareness around all of the things this pocket computer can accomplish and with no extra software other than what Apple provides. There might be three or four alternatives to the solutions I present, but my goal is to put the native functionality first.

You'll notice a lot of words are in bold. This is to help call attention to the app, section, button, menu or toggle you should be looking out for. When you see things like **Settings** > **General** > **About**, this is the order in which you choose these items as you make your way through menu screens. So in this example, you would open the Settings app, then tap the section labeled General, then on the next screen tap the section for About.

This book was written for iOS 12. Some of the exact functionality mentioned could change in a future software update from Apple, but the basics of the tips should stay the same or similar.

A note about 3D Touch and Control Center

As I write this, there are over a dozen iPhone models that support iOS 12. Some have home buttons, others are all touchscreen; some have side buttons, others have power buttons; some support 3D Touch while others use something called Haptic Touch. There are certain models that don't have the functionality at all.

I kept this in mind as I wrote these tips, but instead of explaining how to do each function on every phone model every time, there are a few basics you should know.

When I refer to 3D Touch, this requires a slightly harder press of the screen. It will usually bring up added functionality or an additional menu. iPhone 6s was the first to support it.

One new model that doesn't have 3D Touch is the iPhone XR. This uses something called Haptic Touch, which functions with a similar hard press of the screen but doesn't work everywhere. You can only get the functionality on the lock screen and on Control Center. I have a feeling it will make its way to App shortcuts, but until then, be aware of that as you read these tips that call for a 3D Touch.

Finally, I often refer to Control Center. You can access this by swiping down from the upper right-hand corner of phones without a home button. If your phone has a home button, you can swipe up from the bottom of the screen to bring it up.

Now, let's get to those *101 Handy Tech Tips for the iPhone*.

PART 1

What's New in iOS 12

1

Create a Memoji that looks just like you

New in iOS 12 is the ability to create a virtual animated character that looks just like you. Apple calls it a Memoji, and once you build it you can have a lot of fun using it to send messages with your voice to friends, using it as your head in FaceTime and more.

Keep in mind, to set up a Memoji, you will need an iPhone that has Face ID. It uses this complex camera system to scan your face and follow your movements. Don't worry, you can still send your finished Memoji to anyone you want!

To create a Memoji, go into **Messages** and compose a new message.

Cancel   Done

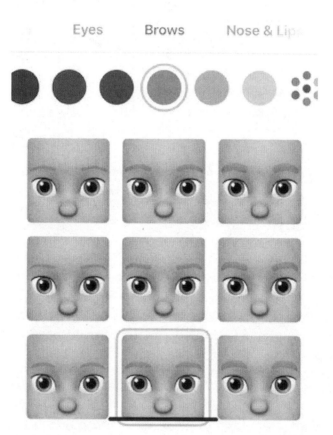

Creating a Memoji

Under the box where you would normally enter your text message, look for the little icon that has a monkey in it and tap it.

This will bring up the Animoji tool. Swipe right until you reveal a big plus sign with "New Memoji" under it.

Tap here to start creating your personalized character. It doesn't necessarily have to look like you, you can really create anything you want!

Start by choosing a skin color, then tap Hairstyle to bring up your options in that department, then swipe left on Hairstyle to move to eyes, brows, nose & lips, ears, facial hair, eyewear and finish with headwear.

You'll notice if you have your phone aimed at your face that your Memoji comes to life, mimicking your every move and expression as you build it.

Hit Done in the upper right-hand corner when you're finished, and your Memoji now appears in the list of Animoji you can use in Messages and FaceTime.

And if you were thinking that the iPhone would create your own likeness just by aiming its camera at your face, nope. This is an avatar that you build yourself. Maybe in the next version of iOS, they'll create a base Memoji for you that you can tweak.

You can build several Memoji if you'd like. If you want to change, delete or duplicate one of your creations, just select it from the row of Animoji's and tap the button that appears in the lower left-hand corner with the three little dots.

You can even sync your Memoji across your iOS devices. Just go into **Settings** > **Apple ID** (the one with your name and picture at the top) > **iCloud** and be sure **iCloud Drive** is switched on.

If you'd like to use your Memoji in iMessage or FaceTime, see the tip about Adding fun camera effects in iMessage and FaceTime.

2

Take control of your notifications

A new feature in iOS 12 lets you better manage the delivery of your Notifications, and you can do it right from a notification itself!

If you bring up your notifications and then swipe right to left on one, you'll notice a new button labeled **Manage**.

Tap it and you'll have some new options available to you. The first is handy if you like getting notifications from a particular app but you don't need your phone to make a big deal out of it. Tap **Deliver Quietly** and notifications from that app will still show up in your list of notifications, but they won't light up your lock screen, make a sound or show a banner while you're using your phone.

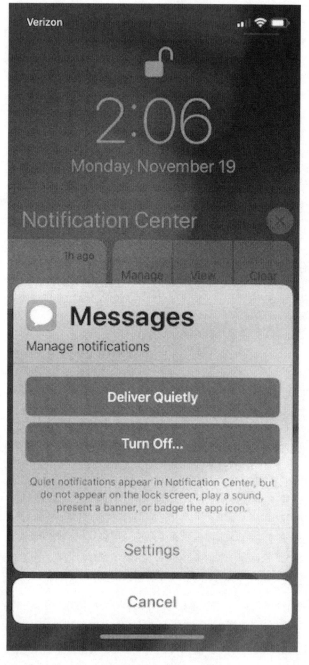

Manage settings right from a notification

Additionally, the App icon won't show a badge with the number of unread notifications in red.

This is level one of "out of sight, out of mind."

Sure, you'll still see the notifications from that app when you check your notification screen, but you won't be interrupted by this app in any meaningful way. It's handy when you don't want to completely forget about an app but you don't need it in your face with every notification.

The next option is **Turn Off**...

This is the more severe option for an app. It will banish all notifications from that app completely. This is for when an app really annoys you with its constant notifications and you just can't take it anymore.

You will never see another notification from that app again unless you turn them back on.

Finally, if you want some more granular control over the notifications sent by a particular app, hit the final option for Settings.

This will take you to what should be a familiar Notifications screen for this particular app. You can now adjust exactly how you get notifications from this app, including the ALERT style, sounds, badges and even whether notifications from this app are shown in CarPlay.

This screen isn't new, but being able to access it in this more streamlined way right from a notification itself is a huge improvement for iOS. I mean, when was the last time you actually went into your apps, one by one, and adjusted their notification settings?

This way, if an app is really bugging you, you can hop into

this screen right from its last notification and nip the problem in the bud.

There is one more option to take a look at in the notifications option screen.

It's the new one under **OPTIONS** labeled **Notification Grouping**. This is a new feature in iOS 12 that will "stack" notifications from the same app on top of each other. You can tap to expand them. You have the option to let your iPhone handle the grouping on a case by case basis, always have notifications grouped by app, or have grouping turned off completely if you like to see each and every one of your notifications all by themselves.

3

See how much you use your phone with Screen Time

Screen Time is a new feature for iOS 12 and it is packed with a lot of information and settings. It's all in an effort to help us spend either less time on our devices or more meaningful time on our devices.

Since this is the first time Apple is including such a complex set of restrictions and timers on their devices, I have a feeling this feature will evolve as time goes on.

There are several ways you can use Screen Time. The first is just to understand how often you are on your phone and which apps you use the most. You can also use this data to set time limits on the apps you use or schedule some time where your phone doesn't do much at all.

Yep, with Screen Time you can literally turn your phone back into a flip phone of yesteryear – so you can make calls and maybe send texts, but not much else.

Let's take a look at the basic Screen Time metrics, which slice and dice how you use your phone.

To find Screen Time, go into **Settings** > **Screen Time**.

Immediately, you will see how long you've used your phone for the day, along with a breakdown of the types of apps you've been using and how this time compares to your average.

You can tap the name of a device to take a deeper dive and see a bigger breakdown. There's a bar chart that maps out your usage along hours of the day, along with your most used apps, how often you pick up your phone and how many notifications you are getting.

Personally, I wouldn't worry too much about **Today**, but I would look at the number for the **Last 7 Days**. You can toggle at the top of the screen.

All of this information is actionable, and you can adjust things by tapping on any app name. If you notice that a social media app is your most used app and you want to limit the time you spend on that app, you can tap its name and scroll down to where it says "Add Limit" to add a daily time limit for that specific app.

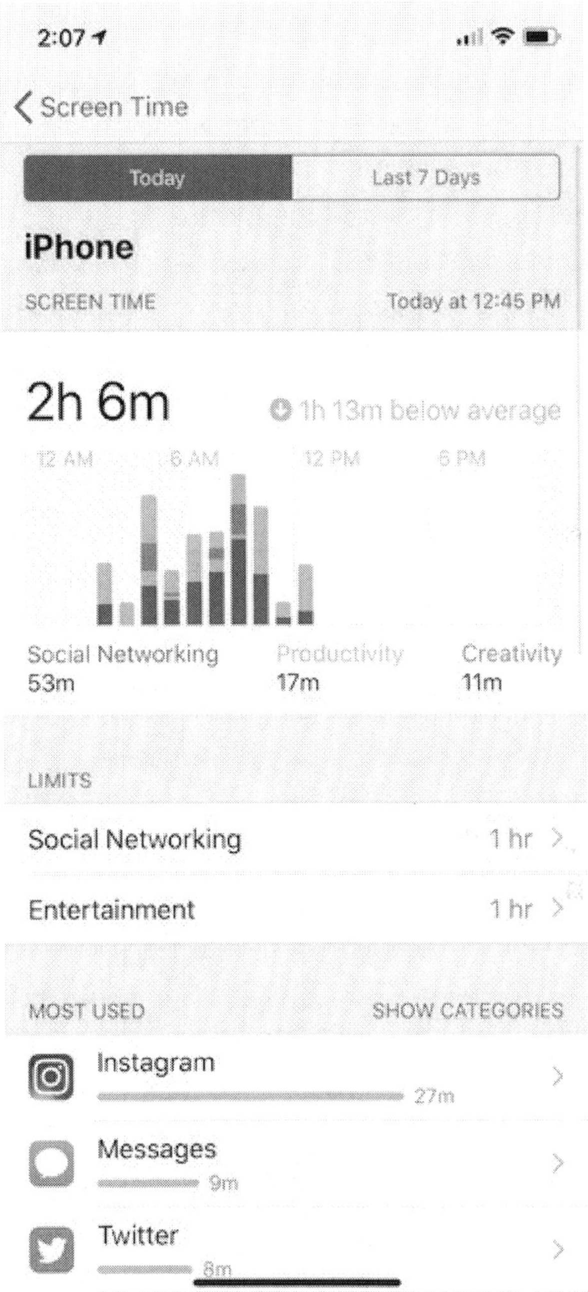

2:07

‹ Screen Time

| Today | Last 7 Days |

iPhone

SCREEN TIME   Today at 12:45 PM

2h 6m   ⊙ 1h 13m below average

12 AM   6 AM   12 PM   6 PM

Social Networking   Productivity   Creativity
53m   17m   11m

LIMITS

Social Networking   1 hr ›

Entertainment   1 hr ›

MOST USED   SHOW CATEGORIES

Instagram
──────────────────────────── 27m   ›

Messages
──────── 9m   ›

Twitter
────── 8m   ›

See how much you use your phone with Screen Time

You can also adjust notification preferences for individual apps from here as well. Tap the name of an app under Notifications and you're taken to a screen where you can turn off or limit notifications from that app.

For instance, the app sending me the most notifications is Twitter, at an average of 85 last week, which is even more than my text messages. If I tap the app name, I'm taken to a screen where I can turn off notifications altogether, change the type of alert I get, or turn off sounds and badges. Don't want any more notifications from that particular app? Just toggle the big switch at the top and they're gone.

4

Set up Do Not Disturb

It might seem counterintuitive, but Do Not Disturb has become one of the handiest features on the iPhone. Admit it, you're drowning in notifications and they interrupt you during every activity – even sleep!

I did a TV segment where we interviewed teenagers and I couldn't believe that many of them told me they leave their phone chirping with notifications all night long – even while they try to sleep!

Apple has made many improvements to Do Not Disturb in iOS 12, but you have to set it up so it works properly.

First, let me explain what Do Not Disturb is. When it's turned on, only the calls and texts you want to receive will come through and ring your phone. You can use it while you sleep, are in a meeting or just want to finish writing a book without interruption. Maybe that last one is just me.

Lots of people are hesitant to set up Do Not Disturb because they fear they will miss out on an important alarm to wake them up or an emergency phone call. Set up properly, you can still let these interruptions in while keeping the rest out.

New in iOS 12 is the ability to set Do Not Disturb to expire after a certain amount of time, when you leave a location or when a calendar event such as a meeting is finished.

There is also a new Bedtime mode that will dim your screen at night when Do Not Disturb is enabled. Also, your iPhone won't show any notifications even if you turn on the screen. This is to prevent you from waking up in the middle of the night and sneaking a peek at your phone screen and then stressing about that notification from your credit card that your bill is due in 7 days. Don't worry, you can see the notifications you missed when Bedtime mode expires.

To set up Do Not Disturb, go into **Settings** > **Do Not Disturb**. Personally, I find it best to use a schedule to turn this feature on and off. Toggle the switch next to Scheduled to turn it on, then choose your quiet hours by tapping the From and To area. Ideally, you would choose a time frame that is a bit before bed and a bit after you normally wake up.

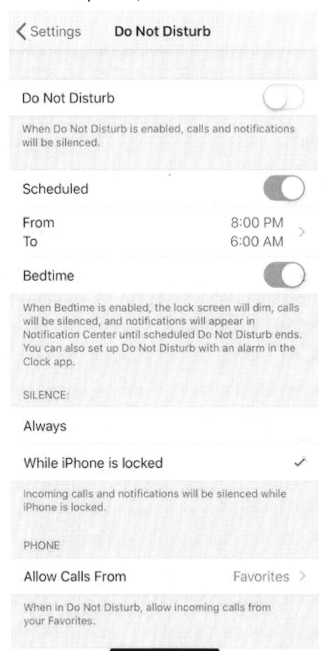

Adjusting Do Not Disturb settings

Once you've chosen your times, back out of that screen and then toggle the switch next to Bedtime to activate that feature as well so your screen dims out and hides your notifications while you get some sleep.

There are two more important options I recommend setting up. The first is labeled "Allow Calls From." Tap in here to set your options. I go with Favorites since these are my closest family and friends. If they call at any time, I'd like the call to ring my phone. You can check to see who your favorites are by going into the Phone app and taping the bottom section with a star where it says Favorites.

The final setting to check is the "Repeated Calls" toggle. I like to turn this on. Basically, if someone calls twice within three minutes, their second call will ring your phone. Don't want to get morbid here, but if someone really needs to get a hold of you for some reason, chances are they will call you again in a short period of time. This allows them to "break through" the Do Not Disturb setting. It's a good idea to turn this on.

Once you're finished setting things up, Do Not Disturb will activate at the scheduled time each night. You can also turn on the feature manually.

From your home screen, bring up control center and look for the crescent-shaped moon. This is the symbol for Do Not Disturb. Tap it once to highlight it and turn the feature on. 3D Touch and you'll get an extended menu with additional options. From here, you can turn the feature on for a certain amount of time, until you leave a location or when a scheduled meeting ends. You might see some or all of these options depending on the time of day.

Keep in mind, you can always manually toggle Do Not Disturb off at any time by returning to the Control Center and tapping the moon so it's no longer lit up.

5

Set up time limits for apps

Now that you have an idea of how long you are spending inside certain apps, you might want to set up time limits so you can limit the amount of time you get to use these apps on a daily basis.

There are no hard and fast rules about this stuff. In fact, the entire digital wellbeing concept is relatively new. It's all about what you believe are healthy limits for yourself. The numbers you saw in Screen Time earlier might either make you feel better or worse about how much you use your phone.

For instance, when this feature came out I immediately set a one-hour time limit for all social networking apps. To my surprise, I don't reach this limit on a daily basis. There are some days when I reach it first thing in the morning and other days when it gets me to just before bedtime. Just like anything else, moderation is key.

Also, just because you set a limit now doesn't mean you can't go in and change it later. Screen Time is just one tool to help you use your phone mindfully.

The other side of all of this is setting up limits for your kids. I'll discuss that in another tip.

First, let's deal with ourselves.

Go to **Settings** > **Screen Time** > **App Limits**.

If you've never set a time limit, the only thing you should see on screen is "Add Limit."

Tap in here and you'll get a list of all of your app categories, like Social Networking, Games, Entertainment, Creativity, Reading & Reference and others.

Choose a category, like Social Networking, then hit the Add button in the upper right-hand corner of your screen.

From here, you'll be able to set a time limit for this group of apps. Keep in mind, the time limit applies to all of your devices signed in with the same iCloud account. You could have an iPhone and an iPad, using Facebook on either would count towards your time limit.

< App Limits **Social Networking**

Time   1 hr

57
58
0   59
1 hour   0 min
2   1
3   2
4   3

Customize Days   >

App limits apply to all devices that are using iCloud for
screen time. A notification will appear five minutes
before the limit expires.

APPS & CATEGORIES

 Social Networking
LinkedIn, Buffer, and 9 more

Edit Apps

Delete Limit

Setting time limits for certain apps

Once you set a time limit, you'll have a new option to "Customize Days." Tap it to adjust your time limits for each day of the week. Perhaps you want less social networking on the weekends – you could lower your time limit for Saturday and Sunday.

I know what you're thinking... this is a lot of work! It sort of is, but again, a lot of us are struggling with how much we use our phones, and generally, it's out of habit. These time limits are just enough to help us put an end to mindless scrolling. I've found that I feel better knowing that I have a certain limit each day. After I'm done with that limit I only extend my time if I really need to, like if I'm at a special event and need access to my social networking apps.

Once you've chosen your time limits and days, the timer is set. You can go back to the categories screen and add another set of limits for another group of apps. If you group categories together, the time limit will apply to apps in all of those categories.

Keep in mind these limits are for the group as a whole. If you choose 1 hour for social networking apps, you don't get 1 hour to use each individual app. You get 1 hour to use all of the apps.

So you might be wondering, wait a second, how do I add a time limit for a specific app? This is done from the main Screen Time stats screen. Go to **Settings** > **Screen Time** and tap the numbers you see for a device under SCREEN TIME.

This will take you to a screen with lots of stats and a list of your most used apps. Tap an app name on this list and all the way at the bottom of the detail page for that app you will see an option for "Add Limit." You can add a time limit for an individual app or multiple apps from here.

So what happens when you hit your time limit for a particular app or category of apps? Just like in Downtime, they become greyed out and unable to use. Don't worry, you can still use the app if you really need to. If you tap it you will get options to use it for another 15 minutes or to ignore the time limit completely for that specific app for the rest of the day.

You also have the option to set up a Screen Time Passcode. If you turn this on, you can set a 4 digit code that must be entered to bypass the time limits when they expire.

Are you thinking what I'm thinking? Yep, these controls can really come in handy for kids devices. Let's explore that concept in the next chapter.

6

Set screen time and content limits for your kids

You may or may not like the idea of screen time limits for yourself, but they can certainly come in handy for dealing with kids eyeballs glued to the screen.

When I was a kid, we just played Nintendo until our thumbs hurt, and that's when we knew it was time to come upstairs and get some fresh air.

With an iPhone in pocket at all times or an iPad with a seemingly endless stream of Netflix to watch, it can be tough to monitor consumption at all times.

Cancel

Screen Time

Get insights about your screen time and
set limits for what you want to manage.

Weekly Reports
Get a weekly report with insights
about your screen time.

Downtime & App Limits
Set a schedule for time away from
the screen and set daily time
limits for app categories you want
to manage.

Content & Privacy Restrictions
Restrict settings for explicit
content, purchases and
downloads, and privacy.

Screen Time Passcode
Manage screen time for children
from your own iPhone, or use a
screen time passcode on your
child's device.

Continue

Turning on Screen Time for family members

That's where Screen Time limits for family members come in handy.

To set them up, go to **Settings** > **Screen Time** and look for the section labeled FAMILY. If you've set up family sharing, you should see any family members on your iCloud account here.

Tap the name of a family member to get started, then choose the option to "Turn on Screen Time."

Once you confirm your choice, you'll be able to get weekly reports about their screen time, set Downtime and App Limits and restrict what they can do – such as downloads and purchases – on their device. It's a powerful tool and yep, your kids probably won't like it.

Additionally, you can set a passcode so your kids can't get around the app time limits or remove them all together.

The first option you'll be presented with is the **Downtime** option. You can set quiet hours for their device where only the apps you choose will continue to work. You can choose times on this screen, or skip the setting for now.

The next screen helps you set **App Limits**. Choose an app category or several, then a daily time limit.

Finally, you can choose to restrict content and other privacy settings on the device. You will be asked to create a passcode. Don't forget it – you'll need it to change any of your settings.

Once things are set up for the first time, you can now go in and tweak individual settings. Keep in mind, to set up individual app times, your child will first have to use those apps so they show up in the Screen Time report.

Also, if you used to restrict certain things on your child's device like Mail, Safari, the Camera or AirDrop, you can find those toggles under the Content & Privacy Restrictions.

I recommend turning these on and going through each setting individually.

Things to pay close attention to?

The ability to make iTunes and In App Purchases and apps you might want to turn off completely like Safari, FaceTime or AirDrop. Additionally, check under Content Restrictions so you can choose an appropriate rating level for your child or block access to web content including adult websites.

There are a lot of settings in here, take your time to go through them all and choose what's appropriate for your child.

One more setting on the main Screen Time screen for your child's device to consider is the option to "Include Website Data." Toggle this on to include the time your child spends on websites in the Screen Time data. It could be handy to know if they are spending long amounts of time on any particular site.

By the way, when your child reaches the time limit on any particular app, they can request an extension in two ways. They can send you a request via notification which you can approve from your device. Or you can manually enter the Screen Time Passcode you chose earlier to give them some more time. You can approve the time limit for 15 minutes, an hour or the entire day.

Of course, you do have one final option available to you, and that is to deny their request completely.

7

Set up Downtime so you can focus

Downtime is another feature new to the iPhone with iOS 12. It's part of the Screen Time functionality and at first glance, it seems like another version of Do Not Disturb.

That's sort of true, it does limit notifications while it's on, but it can be much more powerful.

Downtime can actually limit the functionality of your phone for a certain time period each and every day.

Let's say you want to spend uninterrupted time with your kids from 5 to 7 PM each night. You can use Downtime to schedule your iPhone to go into a mode where apps don't send you notifications AND they won't even work. By default, when you turn this setting on, only the Phone, Messages, FaceTime and Maps will work, but you can choose whichever apps you want to work during Downtime.

To set up Downtime, go to **Settings > Screen Time > Downtime**.

Once you toggle the switch on, you'll see options to set a Start and End time. From our example above, let's set some Downtime from 5 to 7 PM.

Keep in mind, Downtime limits apply to all of your devices signed into the same iCloud device. This will keep you from putting down your iPhone just to pick up your iPad. You'll get a 5-minute warning on your screen before the scheduled Downtime goes into effect.

Once Downtime begins, apps on your phone will be greyed out and a little timer will appear next to their name. If you try to tap a deactivated app, you'll get a notice that says "Time Limit – You've reached your time limit on this app."

There is also an option to "Ignore Limit," if you tap it you'll be presented with an option to use the app for 15 minutes, or you can ignore the limit for the rest of the day.

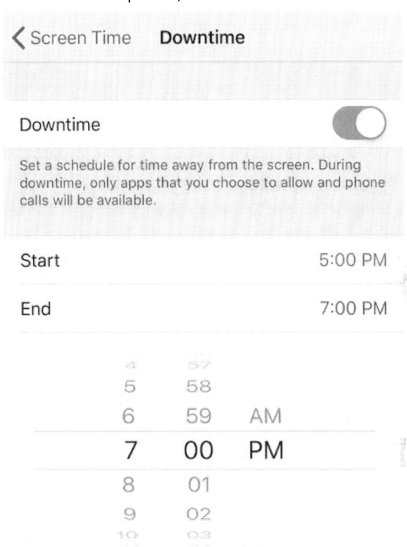

‹ Screen Time   **Downtime**

Downtime

Set a schedule for time away from the screen. During downtime, only apps that you choose to allow and phone calls will be available.

Start   5:00 PM

End   7:00 PM

4	57	
5	58	
6	59	AM
7	**00**	**PM**
8	01	
9	02	
10	03	

Downtime will apply to all devices that are using iCloud for screen time. A downtime reminder will appear five minutes before downtime.

Downtime can help you stay focused

Again, by default just about every app except Phone, Messages, FaceTime and Maps is disabled on your device when you first set up Downtime, but you can go in and choose which apps you'd like to "whitelist," that is, make them so they're always available, even when you're phone is in Downtime mode.

It might be important to you to have WhatsApp or Facebook Messenger or Duo always available. To choose which apps you want to work, go back to the main Screen Time screen by going to **Settings** > **Screen Time** > **Always Allowed**.

From here, you can see the list of apps that are always allowed to function. You can press the minus button to remove apps from the list or press the plus button to add apps to the list.

Try adding an app from the list and then looking at that app on your home screen. You'll notice it's no longer greyed out.

Downtime isn't going to strictly prohibit you from using your phone, but you can use it to so you're less distracted by your device.

8

Add Google Maps or Waze to CarPlay

I know I said that this book primarily deals with first-party apps and features built into the iPhone and not third-party apps, but this is too good to leave out.

In the last version of the book, I chided Apple for not including third-party navigation apps in CarPlay. Well, clearly they read my argument and immediately sprang into action to fix this oversight.

I'm happy to report that, in addition to Apple Maps, you can now use Google Maps, Waze and other third-party navigation apps in CarPlay, which is the screen that appears on your dashboard when you connect your iPhone in a supported car. These days, nearly every major automaker is on board.

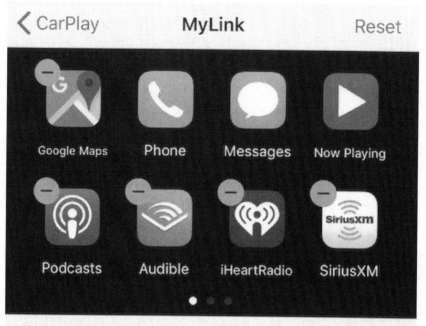

CarPlay now supports third party navigation apps

Even though you have access to this with one of these apps installed, you might not realize it. That's because, by default, the third party map app shows up on a secondary screen on

CarPlay. You have to swipe to see it, and some people might not even think to do this!

Here's how to get your preferred mapping app on the home screen of CarPlay.

Go into **Settings** > **General** > **CarPlay**.

Then, under "MY CAR" tap the appropriate connected car to change.

Here, you will see a little representation what your CarPlay screen looks like when it's on your dashboard. You can now press and hold an icon for a second to pick it up and move it to a new position. Basically, you can rearrange this screen just like you would your iPhone home screen.

Some apps will have little minus signs in a circle, you can tap that icon to remove that app from CarPlay altogether. Don't worry, it's not deleting the app off your phone. It's just hiding it from the CarPlay screen and moving it to a section in this customization screen with inactive apps. If you want it back, just tap the new icon with a plus sign on it to bring it back to the top screen.

If you don't see your preferred mapping app on the CarPlay home page, swipe left on the CarPlay screen. This will reveal another page of apps. You can do this in your car as well.

From here, you can now drag an icon from the second screen to the home screen for easier access in the car.

Now, take a second to rearrange all of your icons to your liking. You'll see the changes the next time you connect your phone in the car.

As you move around and delete apps, you might realize that there are certain, ahem, Apple apps that you can't delete from the CarPlay screen. Apple requires that these items stay there.

You can, however, move them to a secondary screen so they're out of the way if you don't use them very often.

Also, I found out the hard way that you probably don't want to delete Apple Maps altogether off of your phone, even if you're replacing it with another mapping app for navigation purposes. Siri still requires Apple Maps in the car to look up things in the background, like a phone number to a business.

9

Add fun camera effects in iMessage and FaceTime

By now, you're probably used to the concept of adding fun little animations, stickers and text to the photos you post on Instagram Stories, Facebook and other social media platforms.

Now in iOS 12, you can add some similar fun effects using a new tool built right into the camera when you're using iMessage and FaceTime.

You can add Animoji, filters, text, shapes and more with third party sticker packs that appear as you install apps that support the feature.

Fun with Animoji in Messages

To start, go into an iMessage and select one your messages. Make sure it's a friend who doesn't mind getting a goofy picture, just in case you mistakenly send what we're about to create.

Now, look to the left of the area where you normally type in your message – tap the camera icon you see.

Once you're in camera mode, tap the star in the circle, which is located near the shutter button. This will bring up a bunch of fun little tools you can use to add fun elements to your picture.

Let's start with the Animoji. Tap the icon to bring up some fun animated characters. If you've already created a Memoji, you'll see it here too. Choose one and aim the camera at your face. Suddenly, you will see the Animoji take over your head!

Move around and watch how the character mimics your expressions. When you've found one you like, press the X above the row of characters and this will reveal your shutter button. Tap it to take a picture of you as the Animoji.

Once you take the picture, you get some more options to edit it, or you can add even more to your photo using the effects icons. When you're happy with your creation, tap the arrow in the blue circle to send it to your friend instantly.

Yes, I said instantly! Once you tap that blue button with the arrow in it, your picture will be sent without any extra steps to your recipient.

If you don't want to send your picture instantly, tap where it says Done in the upper right-hand corner. This will insert your picture into the message without sending it. This way you can add some text or an explanation. If you change your mind just hit the X in the upper right-hand corner of the picture and it will be deleted.

Just keep in mind that as soon as you hit the shutter button, these pictures are saved in your Camera Roll whether you send them or not.

Go back to the camera and try out the other effects icons. You can add neat looking filters, text, shapes and more depending on the apps you've installed.

You can do the same fun effects in FaceTime too!

Next time you're in a call, tap anywhere on the screen to bring up the same effects button. It's the star in a circle. Tap it to access the same fun camera effects tools you saw earlier in the messages app. Choose a filter or effect, and the person on the other end of your FaceTime will see the effect in real time.

Double tap your own image to make it larger on screen and choose a new effect. If you want to remove the effects completely, just tap the circle in the star again and they will go away.

FYI, to take advantage of these effects you will need an iPhone that supports Face ID. They utilize the same camera to identify your face and follow you around. The person on the other end will still be able to see your effects even if their phone doesn't support creating them.

10

—

Keep connected accessories from stealing your data

If you want to make your iPhone as secure as possible, you probably want to take advantage of a new feature built into the operating system.

It's sort of hidden and confusing, but it's simply labeled USB Accessories. In fact, it might seem counterintuitive to turn it off, but changing this setting can help protect the data on your iPhone from unauthorized access when you plug it into an accessory or computer.

You will have to unlock your phone first before it

communicates with the device. This is important for several reasons. Let's say someone has a tool that can read the data on your iPhone when it's plugged into it. Although it would still be challenging to access, they might be able to do it if the phone communicates with that tool.

This toggle prevents the phone from even communicating with that tool in the first place since your phone is saying "not so fast, my owner hasn't unlocked me." It's only after you unlock the phone that it will send data back and forth through USB connected devices.

Another example: I often get people asking me if they plug their phone into a random USB charging port at the airport, can their data be stolen off of the phone. The short answer is, potentially. Any time you plug your phone into another device, or in this case, what seems to be a USB charging port, there is always a chance that someone has compromised that access point.

It's possible, but not probable. Of course, in the world we live in, with cyber crimes happening nonstop, it's always a good idea to protect yourself. There is a lot of personal information stored on your phone, and it's best to keep it as secure as possible.

To find this setting, go into **Settings** > **Face ID** & **Passcode** and scroll down until you see the section labeled ALLOW ACCESS WHEN LOCKED.

In here, you'll see an option at the bottom for "USB Accessories." If you toggle this option off, it means that you will have to unlock your phone before it will communicate with an accessory that you plug it into.

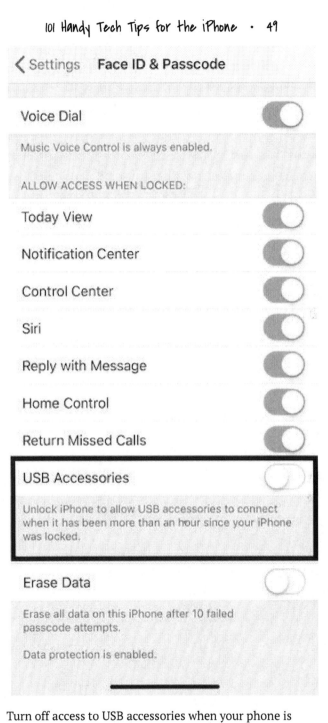

Turn off access to USB accessories when your phone is
locked for added security

Additionally, there is a one hour lockout time. If you haven't unlocked your phone in an hour, it will ask you to unlock it before it will communicate with the device you're plugging it into. This includes your computer, whether it's Mac or PC.

It's really not a big deal in the scheme of things, you just might be asked to unlock your phone if you want to transfer some files back and forth or sync it with iTunes (if you still do that sort of thing) but the added layer of security is worth the extra step.

This setting should not interfere when you plug your phone into a standard charger connected to the wall, but there are certain scenarios where it might not charge due to this higher level of security. This is true if you plug your iPhone into your computer's USB port to charge it but haven't unlocked it yet. You will see a little message when you plug it into your computer that says "USB ACCESSORY, Unlock iPhone to use accessories."

Simply unlock your phone and it will begin charging and stay charging.

11

Turn iPhone into a virtual measuring tape

With iOS 12, your iPhone now has a virtual tape measure built in. Except this one won't cut your hands if you retract it too fast, and it can do some things that no typical measuring tape can.

The magic is all inside a new app called **Measure**. It is now pre-installed when you download iOS 12. Measure uses augmented reality (AR) to figure out the length and dimensions of objects.

To start, open up the app and follow any instructions that appear on the screen. You might need to find and scan a surface or move your phone around a bit. This is to give the app a bit some reference on the nearby areas so it can properly measure things. Don't worry too much about how it works, but just be amazed that some really smart people programmed this stuff to make our lives easier.

Once you see a circle with a little dot in the middle, you're ready to measure.

Aim your phone at something, then tap the plus sign to add a marker. This is the first edge of the item you're measuring. Now, move your phone to the other side of whatever you're measuring and use the plus sign to add another marker.

Measure items virtually

Instantly, you'll see a measurement reading on screen. You can tap the number to see it both bigger and in centimeters. You'll also get an option to copy the measurement, which is handy for saving it to a note or texting it to someone.

Additionally, you can add a second measurement to your object. Just tap the plus sign again and start a new measurement. If you want to do say, the length and width of something, you will need to make sure your second measurement starts at a point on the first line you drew. Otherwise, when you place your second line it will clear out the first one.

Basically, if the measurement lines connect at some point, they will all remain on screen, if they don't, the older lines will disappear when you draw a new one.

You can also change the landing point of your measurements. Just drag one of the dots to a new area on the object and they will "stay" there for the new measurement.

If you make a mistake or want to go back, just press the back button to erase your last move, or the Clear button to start over.

When you're happy with your measurement(s), you can use the capture button to save your work. This looks like a camera shutter button, it's located in the corner of the screen. Tap it and you'll now have a nice picture of the object you just measured, along with the dimensions virtually overlayed on top.

There's one more fun trick you can try with the Measure app. It automagically recognizes squares and rectangles. This way you don't have to go through the entire measurement process. Just place a square or rectangle object in front of the Measure viewfinder and wait until it recognizes the shape. It will let you know it recognizes it when the edges highlight in yellow.

Now, you can tap the plus sign and it will automatically draw the lines, label their dimensions and even give you the square inches or meters of the item.

12

AutoFill Passwords

It's time to stop using the same password for every site that you visit, and before you give me the excuse that it's just too darn tough to do that, let me tell you that the iPhone makes it easier than ever to use a random, unique password for every website you log into.

In fact, the iPhone has had the ability to generate passwords and store them for some time, but in iOS 12 the feature is even better, plus there is support for third-party password managers.

Once you turn this feature on, whenever you go to log into an app or website on your iPhone, it will literally fill in your email or username and password for you instantly. And, it's way more secure than using the same password or variation over and over.

I really don't care if you use the built-in password management system, called iCloud Keychain, or a third party app like LastPass, Dashlane or 1Password, but I want you to use one and stick with it.

Believe me, I've heard all of the excuses. It's too complicated. It's too much effort. I can't remember. Hackers don't care about me. I don't have anything to hide/lose/worry about. All of these excuses are wrong.

If you were to be hacked, you would absolutely be affected and it would not be fun to try to pick up the pieces of your online life. I've done stories with folks who lost access to their Instagram account and they're devastated. Really. It's an invasion of your personal space in a way that you can't really explain until it happens to you.

And if you think it's easy to just contact Google, Amazon, Facebook, Instagram, your bank, credit card and others to recover from a hacked account, think again. It will consume your life.

OK, I hope that convinced you.

First, you need to pick your ally in this war against hackers. You can start with the built-in password management system on iPhone if you don't feel like making things complicated.

Basically, every time you are presented with an option to create or change a password, your iPhone will spring to life to assist you. Then it will save the password and enter it automatically when you need to log in again.

The main downside to using the built-in iCloud Keychain is that it only works on Apple devices: iPhone, iPad, Mac Computers, etc. If you are 100% Apple, this isn't a big deal, but if you mix and match devices it's a dealbreaker.

Your other option is to choose one of the third-party apps I mentioned earlier. Of the bunch, LastPass is free, but the others will charge you for a yearly membership. Do some research and figure out which option is best for you, then you can set up AutoFill Passwords.

You'll find this option under **Settings** > **Passwords & Accounts**.

On this screen, tap the area where it says AutoFill Passwords, then on the next screen, toggle the switch to turn the option on.

Now, you'll see a new section labeled ALLOW FILLING FROM: along with one or multiple choices, depending if you've installed a third-party app such as Dashlane or 1Password.

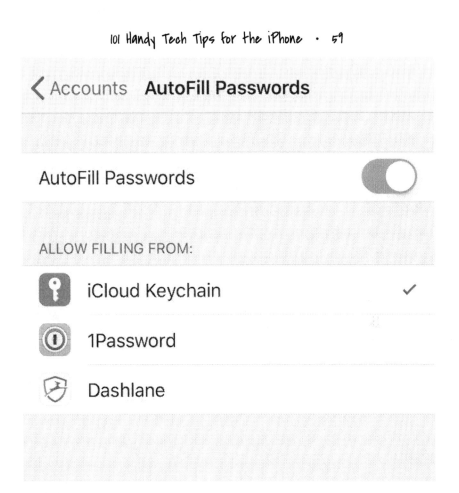

Choose a password helper and stick with it

Tap the password manager you want to use and back out of the screen to save your settings.

Now, open Safari and navigate to a page where you would normally log in, like Facebook.com. (if you're already logged in, log out just to see how this works)

Tap in the password field and you'll see a new option above your keyboard that says Passwords. Tap it and you'll get an option to autofill your Facebook password or generate a new, secure one.

My advice – once you set up this Autofill feature, take some time to do a password reset on some of your most visited sites and let the iPhone (or your preferred app) generate a new, secure password and save it for you.

The next time you go to log into that website or app your iPhone will automatically fill in your username and password for you. You don't even have to remember a thing.

I know it's a few extra steps to accomplish this, but believe me, the extra protection of your accounts is worth it.

13

Group FaceTime with up to 32 People

FaceTime got a FaceLift in iOS 12. Not only are the onscreen controls a bit different, but there is a new feature called Group FaceTime that lets you have up to 32 people in one Group FaceTime call!

That might be handy for a business meeting, but for the rest of us, we might like the option to FaceTime with just a few of our closest family members or friends all at once.

To make it happen, just start a **FaceTime** call as usual, then the button with the three little dots in it. If you don't see it onscreen, just tap anywhere on the screen to bring it up.

From here, you should see an option to **Add Person**.

Tap and type in the person's contact info, then tap the

option to "Add Person to FaceTime." Repeat this process until you have up to 31 of your closest friends and family on the same call.

You can also start a Group FaceTime from the Messages app. Just open up a group conversation you've already been chatting in.

Then, tap the icons at the top of the message that contains everyone's profile pictures or initials.

You'll see an option for FaceTime. Tap it to IMMEDIATELY start a Group FaceTime video chat. Again, there is no confirmation here. Once you tap, the call will initiate.

As you video chat, the system will attempt to understand who is talking and display their video more prominently on the screen.

Keep in mind that not every model of iPhone or iPad supports the Group FaceTime functionality. According to Apple, you'll need an iPhone 6s or later, iPad Pro or later, iPad Air 2 or iPad Mini 4, all running iOS 12.1 or later. Other devices can still join but they will simply be audio participants as opposed to video.

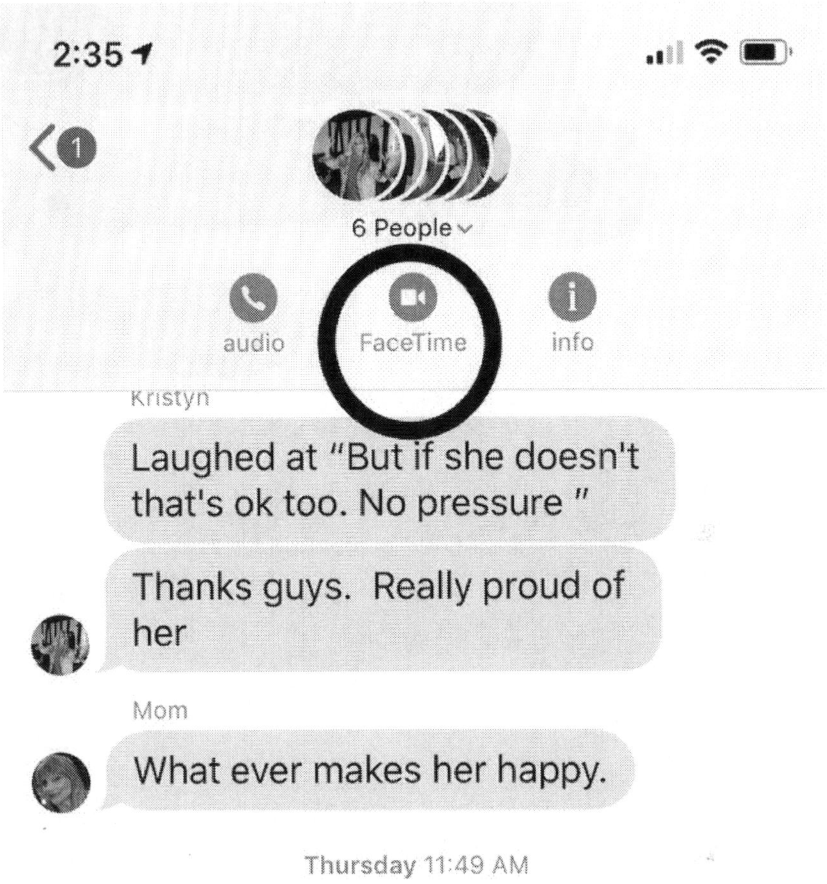

Tap to start a group FaceTime call fast

14

Capture a FaceTime memory with a screenshot

Between traveling for my job and my family living on the East Coast, I'm often on FaceTime video chatting. For some reason, there always seems to be a special moment I want to capture while we're virtually face to face.

For a short time, iOS had a screenshot functionality built into FaceTime, but that no longer seems to be the case.

Don't despair, you can still capture a FaceTime memory by taking a screenshot the old-fashioned way.

Just quickly press the side button and volume up button

simultaneously on iPhones without a home button, or the power button and the home button simultaneously on iPhones with a home button.

The screenshot will show both parties, which is fun for memory keeping.

I have some great FaceTime screenshots from years back when my first kid was just a little tot and I was traveling on business. It's so fun to have those memories saved forever in my photos library.

15

Use Siri Shortcuts to save time and taps

History will tell if Siri Shortcuts are the best thing to ever happen to Siri or just a passing fad. Siri Shortcuts are tasks that you program into Siri yourself, complete with a phrase you record that triggers them.

For instance, let's say I want to navigate to work each day but I don't feel like saying, "Siri, navigate to 123 Main Street" each and every day. I can program a Siri Shortcut to navigate to my preferred address just by saying "Siri, let's rock and roll."

There are plenty of other uses for Siri Shortcuts, and more are being added each and every day as developers update their apps to take advantage of the new functionality.

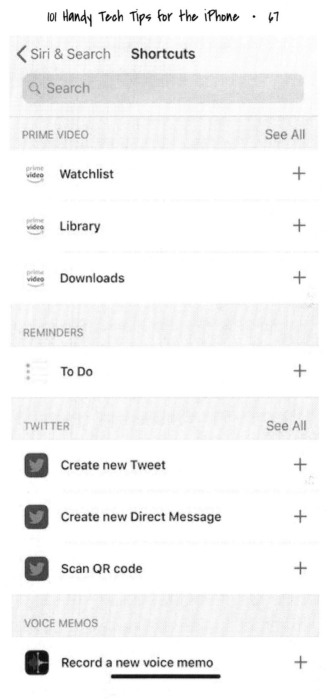

Siri Shortcuts can save you time

That's why I said it could be the best thing to ever happen to Siri. Think about it. In the past, everything that Siri was able to accomplish had to be built in and hard-coded by Apple's engineers.

Now, individual apps can add functionality to Siri with a few lines of code. This means Siri can be customized to suit your needs more than ever.

Here's how you do it.

Go into **Settings** > **Siri & Search** and look for the section labeled SUGGESTED SHORTCUTS. These are a few ready-made shortcuts Siri thinks you might want to add. They might be just what you're looking for, but you can see a complete list of everything available to you under the section labeled "All Shortcuts."

Tap it and you'll see a list of all of your apps that support Siri Shortcuts, along with the actions they support.

For instance, I have Headspace installed on my iPhone and one of the shortcuts is "Open today's meditation." If I tap that Shortcut, I can now assign any Siri phrase I want to trigger that action.

Once you tap a shortcut, you'll be taken to a screen where you can record your own custom Siri Shortcut phrase. In this example, I'll say something like "Let's meditate," and that will trigger the Headspace app to bring up today's meditation.

However, you can choose any phrase you want! You can say, "Siri, Center me" or "Siri, let's de-stress," or "Siri, my boss is getting on my nerves and I need to relax" and it will trigger the Headspace shortcut you assigned to that phrase.

See the power of this system? The main downside is that you need to remember the phrases that you assigned to the shortcuts or it won't work. Don't worry, you can see all of your phrases later.

For now, press the big red record button and try assigning a phrase to an action. I'll assign "Let's Meditate" to bring up the Headspace daily meditation.

When you're finished, press Done and the newly assigned Siri Shortcut will appear in a list called "My Shortcuts."

Now, let's try out our newly assigned shortcut.

Go to your home screen, activate Siri and say your phrase. For instance, I can now say "Hey Siri, Let's Meditate" and Siri will open up the Headspace app and take me right to the daily meditation. That just saved me several steps.

You can go back into **Settings** > **Siri & Search** > **All Shortcuts** to record more shortcuts for your apps. If you don't see a particular app or shortcut supported, the developers of that app haven't built in that functionality yet. Don't forget to check back though, since more shortcuts are continually being added.

To see a list of all of your shortcuts, go into **Settings** > **Siri & Search** > **My Shortcuts**.

Tap it to see a list of your assigned shortcuts. Swipe left on a shortcut to delete it, or tap to change settings. You can re-record the phrase to use different keywords.

Siri Shortcuts are a potentially powerful new addition to iOS. If you take the time to set up a few useful shortcuts they can really save you some time, or you can just have fun with custom Siri commands.

16

—

Add a second Face ID

Love it or hate it, it seems like Face ID is here to stay. But while you used to be able to add multiple fingerprints from multiple family members to unlock iPhones with Touch ID, Face ID launched with the ability to register one face at a time.

Now, with iOS 12 you can register two faces. This means you can finally have your phone recognize you when you first wake up and then throughout the day!

Just kidding. Face ID actually does learn to recognize the subtleties of your appearance the more you use it, but now you can register a second look in addition to your normal look.

What does this mean? Nobody is really sure, but it could be inspired by clowns, surgical masks, beard growers and anyone else who drastically changes their look throughout the day.

Can you register a second face altogether? It seems like you can, so say, a spouse can unlock your phone as well, but it doesn't seem like that's Apple's intention with this new feature. So proceed at your own risk when you add two totally different faces as that could theoretically make the ID less secure.

Here's how to add the second look.

First, go into **Settings** > **Face ID & Passcode**. You'll have to verify yourself by entering your passcode before you can proceed.

Next, tap the area where it says "Set Up an Alternate Appearance." The system will ask you to scan your face a few times and then the feature will be set up.

Once it is, you will notice that you don't have an option to delete one face or the other. If you want to delete data for either Face ID, you'll have to start all over and reset Face ID completely. This makes me believe that Apple doesn't want folks to use this alternative feature to register multiple different faces, but the same face twice for faster and more reliable unlocks for one person.

< Settings   **Face ID & Passcode**

USE FACE ID FOR:

iPhone Unlock

iTunes & App Store

Apple Pay

Password AutoFill

Other Apps   6 Apps >

iPhone can recognize the unique, three-dimensional features of your face to allow secure access to apps and payments. About Face ID & Privacy...

Set Up an Alternate Appearance

In addition to continuously learning how you look, Face ID can recognize an alternate appearance.

Reset Face ID

Give Face ID a second look

17

Delete a used boarding pass

Apple Wallet is a handy way to store all kinds of loyalty cards, gift cards, boarding passing and more. But for some reason, boarding passes seem to linger in there long after your flight is complete.

Here's how to get rid of a boarding pass you've added to Apple Wallet.

First, open the **Apple Wallet** app and look for the boarding pass you would like to delete. Tap it to bring it full screen.

Now, look for the **icon with three little dots** in the lower right-hand corner of the pass and tap it. This will bring up your options for this pass.

Look for the option that says "Remove Pass."

Tap it and watch the pass vanish right before your eyes.

If you're having trouble finding your old passes or the Remove Pass button, it could be because your phone isn't unlocked.

You can't activate your Wallet using the shortcut key and then delete passes. This is for security reasons – if someone got a hold of your phone, they would be able to delete items out of your wallet without unlocking your device. That would not be good.

For this reason, you can only delete passes if you access the Wallet app from your home screen after your phone is unlocked.

18

Automatically name voice memos with location

In iOS 12, Voice Memos got a makeover. This is a handy little app for taking voice notes, recording lectures, creating podcasts and secretly recording conversations with your adversaries to use against them later.

Did I really just put that last one in writing? I'm totally kidding. Voice Memos should never be used for that.

But there is a new feature that can help you organize your notes and find a voice note faster than ever. You can now have Voice Memos automatically assign a name to a note based on the location where you took that note.

To set it up, go into **Settings** > **Voice Memos**.

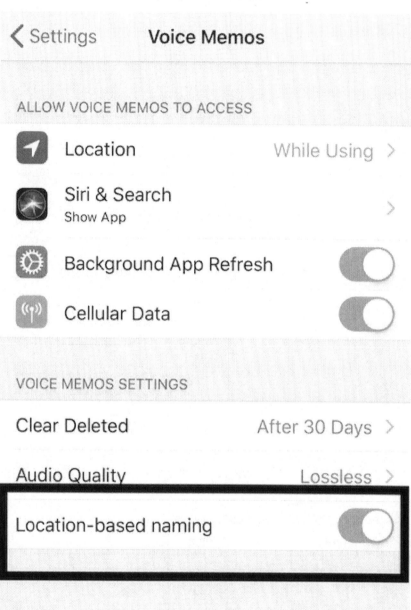

Name Voice Memos with their location

Look for the option for "Location-based naming" and toggle it on. Now, when you take a note somewhere, Apple will use GPS to figure out the location and use the address as the name.

For example, if you record a voice note at 123 Main Street, this will become the name of the note. When you're looking for that note you recorded later on, the title should give you a hint.

This sure beats the old system where notes were pretty much all labeled the same way but with a sequential number at the end. I never took the time to label them, and apparently, no one else did either.

You'll notice when you record a note at Home or Work they'll be labeled that way as well.

If you don't like this new labeling convention and would like to preserve the old "New Recording 75" titles, just go into **Settings** > **Voice Memos** and flip the switch next to Location-based naming.

While we're on the topic of Voice Memos, here are two more quick ways to start a recording.

If you have an iPhone that supports 3D Touch, you can hard press the app icon and this will bring up an option to start a New Recording.

Alternatively, you can add a Voice Memos button to Control Center. Go to **Settings** > **Control Center** > **Customize Controls** and tap the plus sign next to Voice Memos. Back out to save your settings and now you can access Control Center and tap the little icon that looks like an audio waveform to bring up the app.

Keep in mind, this method will not automatically start a new recording when you tap the Control Center button. You'll still need to hit the big red button to start recording.

If you want to instantly start a recording from Control

Center, 3D Touch the icon to bring up the New Recording option. Tap it and the tape will be rolling, so to say. I know, everything is digital these days.

19

Set up a second phone line

The latest iPhones have the ability to have two phone lines on one device. Apple introduced the feature on the iPhone XS, XS Max and the iPhone XR. This has been a longtime feature in other countries around the world, but having the feature on the iPhone is pretty handy.

For instance, you can have both a work line and a personal line on one phone, so one less device to carry around. And before you yell at me and say that there are lots of apps that can add a second line to the iPhone, hear me out.

This feature is actually adding a real, second phone line to the device. Not a virtual line. The number is associated with a SIM card and carrier.

Previous phones accomplished this with two physical SIM card slots that would accommodate two different SIM cards. A SIM card is a tiny little chip that you put inside a phone to identify your phone to the cellular towers. It looks just like the gold chip on your credit card, but with much less plastic surrounding it. It can fit on the tip of your finger.

If you're a real nerd like myself, you have taken these things in and out of phones many times, but if you're a normal person you might have seen the customer service people at AT&T or T-Mobile swap them out from your phone to a new device when you change handsets.

Apple is using a combination of one physical SIM card and one electronic SIM card to accomplish the two phone lines thing. (Unless you're in China, then your phone actually does have space for two physical SIM cards.)

What's cool about this is that you can add a second line to your phone pretty easily for a variety of reasons. Of course, the work and personal line come to mind, but there will be many other opportunities too.

For example, let's say you travel outside the United States often. You can still keep your primary line for use in the United States, but set up a secondary line just for cheaper international data.

Another scenario. Let's say you have your primary line but want a secondary line for your "side hustle." You can quickly add a second line that lets you separate your calls and texts for the side business, and maybe the carrier only charges you $5 a month for it.

As I write this, carriers in the U.S. aren't yet set up for

the electronic activation necessary to add lines on the iPhone instantly, but they will get there.

When they do, here's how to add a second line. Just go into the **Settings** > **Cellular** and look for the option to "Add Cellular Plan." Tap it to activate a camera screen that's used to scan a QR code. This is how the carrier will link your phone with the new line.

Additionally, you'll be able to download a carrier app and set up the line from there and link it to your phone.

Things are about to get interesting with these second lines because it represents a new opportunity for new, virtual carriers to offer deals to entice folks to set up a secondary line.

Once your line is set up, you will notice some small changes in the way your iPhone handles your calls.

For starters, you will have to assign how each line will work. You can choose one line to be a default line that is your primary line for calls and texts, and the other can be a data only line.

You're always free to choose which line to use when you're dialing a number or sending a text. If you have two lines set up on your phone, you'll notice new options for switching between them before you make a call or send a text.

You'll also be able to see the signal status for both lines in Control Center.

If it all sounds super complicated, that's understandable. Like anything else, if you choose to set up a secondary line, you'll get used to it, it's just a matter of being aware of which line you're using to make calls and send texts.

When you're calling back numbers or responding to texts,

they'll always go back through the same number they arrived on.

Apple has more information on the subject here:
https://support.apple.com/en-us/HT209044
https://support.apple.com/en-us/HT209096

PART II

The Essentials

20

——

Take a screenshot

Taking a screenshot is one of the most basic iOS functions. It can come in handy for so many reasons, from mental notes to web clippings, to saving embarrassing texts to talk about later.

To take a screenshot on an iPhone without a home button, all you have to do is press the **Volume Up Button + Side Button** simultaneously.

This is a rapid, firm movement. If you linger too long on either button, you'll turn up the volume, activate Siri or bring up the power off, Medical ID and SOS options.

If your iPhone has a home button, just hit the **Home Button + Power Button** simultaneously.

Again, just a quick push of both buttons at the exact same time and you'll see a flash of white, followed by a little screenshot image in the lower left-hand corner of your screen.

A screenshot of a screenshot

Once you see this thumbnail, you can tap it to bring up additional options to modify it. This way, you can quickly crop it, highlight some text, draw on it, share it and more.

Notice the blue border around your screenshot? Try dragging one of the handles you see on the corners or centered on the sides. Adjusting these instantly crops your photo. You'll see your screenshot grey out while you are adjusting it. Let go and the greyed area is immediately sliced away. Just drag the blue handles out again to get something back.

Once you've made a crop, you can use two fingers to pinch the image to zoom it in or out.

Make a mistake? Just hit the Undo and Redo buttons in the upper right-hand corner of your screen.

You can use the markup tools along the bottom of the screen to write on your screenshot and highlight text. If you want to change the color of your pen, highlighter or pencil, just tap the circle icon to bring up a pallet of available options.

Press the Plus sign to bring up even more options including the ability to add Text, your Signature, shapes, lines or my favorite, a magnifying glass to call attention to a particular area of the screenshot.

I still haven't found a valid use for this one, but I know I will one day, and it will be amazing.

When you're finished with your creation, you have several options available to you. You can tap the Share button to share it out via AirDrop, apps or the system.

You can also tap **Done** to **Save** your screenshot to your Photos to share or access later or **Delete** it all together.

21

Close out apps

Apple must have heard the complaints about how complicated it was to force close out apps in iOS 11, because in iOS 12 it's a whole lot easier.

You used to have to press and hold and then tap and hold until a little icon came up to close out apps, but the steps have been simplified.

Now, to close out apps in iOS 12 it's much more straightforward.

From the home screen, swipe up from the bottom and you'll instantly reveal a bunch of cards that represent all of the apps you have recently used. You can scroll through this cascade of apps by swiping left or right through them.

Swipe up on a recent app to close it out

To close out an app, just swipe up on the card to send it on its way. This will close out the app permanently – handy if it's misbehaving or acting up or otherwise just needs to go away.

Now, before you go closing out all apps right after you use them, hear me out.

For some reason, iPhones users have developed a bad habit of closing out their "unused" apps. I say bad habit because it's been said many times that there is no reason to do this. In fact, closing out old apps could actually use more battery and memory since your phone has to work slightly harder to re-open them and get them started up again.

Keep in mind, the way iOS works is that when you are finished with an app and exit it to return to the home screen, the app gets a bit of time to finish any pending tasks. Then, after a certain period of time, it is put to sleep so it can't do anything else in the background. It might wake up again occasionally as allowedly by the operating system or to continue to stream music, for example, but for the most part, this is all highly regulated by iOS.

It's one of the reasons why battery life is so good on the iPhone – not much is happening in the background when your phone is idle.

Still, there are some legit reasons you might want to "close out" or "force close" an app. It could be misbehaving, crashing or you just hate seeing it in your app history. For any and all of those reasons, you can get rid of recent apps.

Since I know you love to swipe, I'll give you a little hint – you're not limited to one app at a time. Try using a few fingers to close out several apps at once. When you're finished, just tap anywhere on the screen to exit recents mode and bring your phone back to the home screen.

Now that you have the knowledge about power swiping apps away, use it wisely. I know you won't be "one of those" people that just closes out their apps for no good reason, right?

22

Check for app updates

If you're a super nerd like me, you can't wait for the latest software updates to arrive for the apps on your phone. This usually brings bug fixes, and in some cases, added functionality.

To me, it's a little like Christmas every time there's an update available in the App Store for my installed apps.

If you want to use a new feature just added to an app or there's some sort of recurring issue you're having with an app, it's a good idea to check to see if there's a software update available.

To do this, open up the **App Store** and tap the **Updates** section at the bottom of the screen. It might even have a little red number on it. This is how many updates are available for your apps.

Updates

Pending   Update All

Dark Sky Weather
Today   UPDATE

- Daily snow accumulation totals   more

Google Maps -
Transit & Food   UPDATE
Today

Thanks for using Google Maps! This release
brings bug fixes that improve our product   more

Headspace:
Meditation   UPDATE
Today

Sometimes a bug sneaks through the cracks. We
don't like sneaky bugs, so we removed it.   more

Hopper - Book Flights

Today   Games   Apps   Updates   Search

Pull down on the App updates screen to check for updates

But before you hit the **Update All** button, I want you to do one more thing.

"Pull down" on the Updates screen to make sure you really are getting all of the updates currently available to you.

Once you pull far enough, you'll notice a spinning circle icon appear at the top of the screen. Pull down and hold this action until that circle starts to spin continuously, then release the screen.

Now you are ready to update your apps.

Why is this a good idea?

For starters, it usually fixes any issues happening with apps. These are generally referred to as "bugs." Developers are constantly listening to feedback on what works and what's broken inside their apps, so they push out updates to fix little annoying glitches.

Updates also bring about new functionality, and security fixes.

It's a good idea to update your apps regularly. I check this pretty much every day. Then again, I'm a nerd.

One more setting to make life a little easier when it comes to App updates. You can have your phone automatically download the updates as they're available by tweaking a setting.

Go into **Settings > iTunes & App Stores** and under AUTOMATIC DOWNLOADS toggle the switch for Updates. Keep in mind, you'll still have to install the updates, this will just download them in the background when your phone is connected to WiFi.

23

Cancel a subscription

iPhone makes it really easy to subscribe to things. You can have unlimited music, a new magazine each month, videos and so much more with the tap of a fingerprint or a quick Face ID.

Unsubscribing to these things is nearly impossible for the mere mortal.

It shouldn't be this way, but it is – and it's not just Apple. Throughout history, we have seen the ease of subscribing followed by the pain of canceling – remember CD clubs?

Let's take this time to clean house and clear out any old subscriptions lingering in your iTunes account.

First, open the **App Store** on your phone.

Now, tap one of the tabs at the bottom to be sure you're on a "main" section of the store with a circle (it should have your profile picture in it) in the upper right-hand corner.

Account Settings   Done

Personalized Recommendations

When Personalized Recommendations is turned on, your downloads, purchases, and other activity will be used to improve your recommendations on the iTunes Store, the App Store, and Apple Books.

MOVIES ANYWHERE:

Disconnect

Your iTunes account is connected to your Movies Anywhere account. You may only connect one account at a time and switch accounts every 180 days.Movies Anywhere Terms and Conditions

Subscriptions   >

Purchase History   >

ITUNES IN THE CLOUD

Hidden Purchases   >

Unhide purchases that you have previously hidden.

Remove This Device

This device can be used with Automatic Downloads and can also download previously purchased music, apps, movies, TV shows, and books.

Find and manage your subscriptions

This will bring us to your Apple Account.

Tap the circle, then tap where it says your name and email address.

This will take you to your **Account Settings** page.

Scroll about a third of the way down the screen to find the section labeled **Subscriptions** and tap there.

You might need to re-verify your password, but once you do you will see a list of your ACTIVE and EXPIRED subscriptions.

Take a good look at anything listed under ACTIVE subscriptions. You can see the name of the subscription, along with the date you'll be charged for renewal next.

Tap a subscription to investigate further and see the cost and renewal options.

Keep in mind, some subscriptions are cheaper if you prepay them for a longer period of time. So it's often worth visiting this page after you subscribe to anything to see if you can nab a better deal if you don't mind paying more up front.

For instance, after you subscribe to Apple Music, if you check this detail page you'll notice an option to pre-pay for a full year for $99, versus $9.99 a month. That would save you $20 over the course of a year. This book just paid for itself!

Back to the subscription detail page. This is where you will find the option to Cancel Subscription. Under this red text, you'll notice smaller text that lets you see how long you are paid up for – it tells you how long you will have access to a particular subscription even after you cancel it.

This also means that you don't necessarily have to wait until a free trial is over or nearing the end to cancel it. You can cancel your subscription right after you sign up and still use it for the length of the free trial. They're probably hoping you do one of two things – fall in love with the service during the free trial and continue as a subscriber forever. Or two, forget about your free trial end date and get in at least one more charge before you remember to cancel.

If you tap the red **Cancel Subscription** text you'll get a pop-up box confirming your cancellation and one more explainer on just how long your subscription will last until.

That's all there is to it. You never have to wonder where your subscriptions are ever again. Just remember: **App Store, tap your picture, go into your account, scroll down, find Subscriptions and tap there**.

It's maybe just a little bit easier than the CD clubs of yesteryear.

24

Turn off your iPhone

It's pretty crazy to think that something as simple as turning off the iPhone has become so complicated. You see, once upon a time, long long ago, there used to be a dedicated power button on the iPhone. But no more. These days, you'll only find a Siri or "side" button, along with volume keys.

The natural thing to do is press and hold down the side button, but that just activates Siri. Hold it down longer and Siri just says that she is listening. Double press the Siri button and that brings up Apple Pay. Not what you need.

To turn off the iPhone, you need to hold down two buttons at once: **The Siri (or side) button along with one of the Volume buttons**. It doesn't matter which one. Holding down this combination of keys for a few seconds will bring up a new screen with that familiar "slide to power off" slider. Can I call it that? Well, I just did.

Just slide the slider to turn the phone off. When you want to turn the iPhone back on, just press and hold the side button for a bit until the Apple logo appears, then release it.

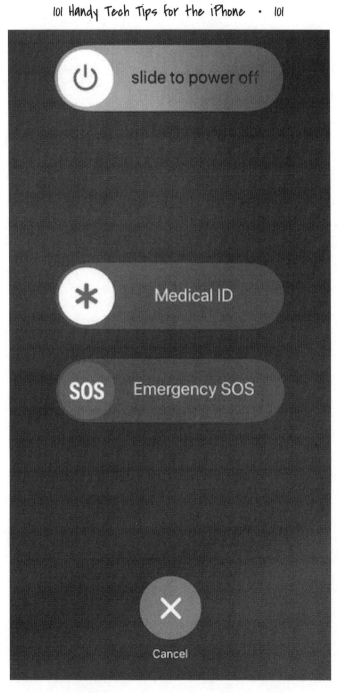

Press and hold the side + volume button to turn off iPhone

PART III

Privacy and Security

25

Make your notifications more private

Notifications on the iPhone can arrive at any time. And, since they light up the screen and show their contents, someone nearby might be able to read what you're being sent.

If it's a sensitive message, it can put you in an awkward situation.

Additionally, someone could pick up your phone and scroll through your notifications while your phone is locked and still see the contents of your messages.

If you're concerned about this or don't like the idea of random people being able to see your stuff, you can change a setting so your iPhone will only show you the contents of a notification after your phone is actually unlocked.

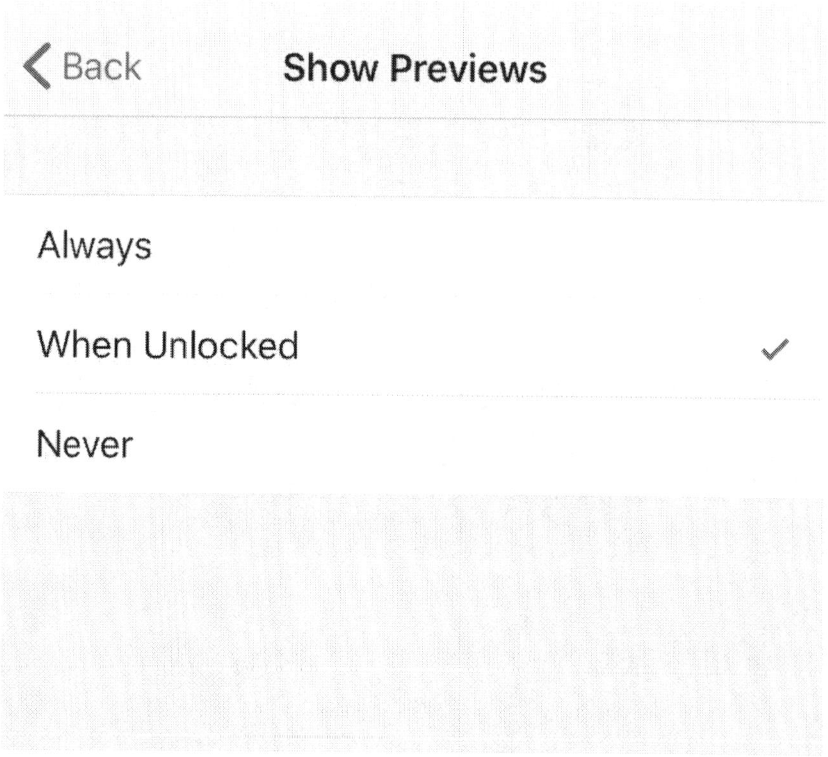

‹ Back   **Show Previews**

Always

When Unlocked   ✓

Never

Change notifications so they only show their contents when your phone is unlocked

To switch to these more secure notifications, go to **Settings > Notifications > Show Previews** and switch to "When Unlocked" or "Never."

"When Unlocked" means someone can see that you have a notification from a particular app when your phone is locked, but they won't be able to see the contents of the notification. It will just say Notification until you unlock your phone, then the message will instantly transform to reveal its contents.

If you choose "Never," your notifications won't ever reveal their contents, even when your phone is unlocked. You'll have to tap a notification to bring you to the app to see what it's all about.

Try it – change your setting to When Unlocked, then ask a friend to send you a text and quickly lock your phone. The notification will come in as usual and light up your phone screen, but instead of displaying the contents of the message, it will only tell you the name of the app sending the notification. It's only when you unlock your phone with your Face or Fingerprint that your messages will be displayed.

Personally, I have my notifications set to show only when my phone is unlocked.

Changing this setting can help you avoid an awkward situation, especially if your spouse or friends are known to send you outrageous messages.

While that's not the case with me, I'd just rather keep my notifications for my eyes only and avoid these scenarios altogether.

26

Set up Two Factor Authentication

Protecting your accounts by all methods possible is more important now than ever before. Hackers are getting more and more sophisticated and you need to use all of the protections available to keep your information safe.

This is a feature that you must absolutely turn on. Don't put it off, don't think you don't need it and don't think it can't happen to you.

Two-factor authentication provides an extra layer of protection on your account to guard against someone else trying to log in, and it's essential to have it on.

Once it's turned on, if someone tries to log into your Apple account from a phone, computer or elsewhere, you'll get a notification with a special code. This code must be entered, or the login cannot proceed.

Turning on two-factor authentication can actually help safeguard you from yourself, too!

For example, let's say you fall victim to one of those phishing emails going around.

They pretend to be from Apple and one of the most convincing looks like it's a receipt for an in-app purchase.

You see it and say, "Wait for a second, I didn't spend $49.99 on 5,000 gold coins in Supermarket Mania!"

Conveniently, there is a link right at the bottom of the receipt that says "click here if you don't recognize this transaction."

You click and the next thing you know, you're brought to an Apple login page. You log in with your email address and password before you realize some words are misspelled, or the web address is slightly off. But by the time you realize your mistake, it's already too late.

Someone on the other end has already sprung into action, using the email and password combo you just handed them! They will immediately try to access your account and do some real damage.

But, if you have two-factor authentication turned on, it would protect you from this scenario because when the scam artists try to log into your account, you'll get a notification on your iPhone that says "so and so is trying to log in from Russia – approve this?"

Clearly, something isn't right, so you can decline the login. You can then go into your account and change your password.

You just avoided a big headache.

< Apple ID   Password & Security

Change Password

Two-Factor Authentication   On

Your trusted devices and phone numbers are used to
verify your identity when signing in.

TRUSTED PHONE NUMBER   Edit

Trusted phone numbers are used to verify your identity
when signing in and help recover your account if you
forget your password.

Get Verification Code

Get a verification code to sign in on another device or at
iCloud.com.

Turn on Two-Factor Authentication for added security

Hopefully, I've convinced you to set up two-factor
authentication. So, grab your iPhone and head to **Settings** and

tap the very top section where it has your name along with Apple ID, iCloud, iTunes & App Store.

Once you're in, tap the section labeled **Password & Security**.

In here, you'll see the option for **Two Factor Authentication**. Tap to set it up.

You'll have to enter a phone number where you can receive a text message or a phone call to verify you. Type in your phone number and choose whether you want to receive a text (easier) or a phone call.

Apple will send a verification PIN to the number that you enter, so be sure it's a nearby phone.

Once you receive the verification code, type it into the screen. You'll get a message from Apple saying to update all of your devices for the best two-factor experience.

Now, you should be back at the Password & Security screen and Two-Factor Authentication should be On!

You'll notice there isn't a way to turn Two Factor off from your iPhone. You'll have to go to a web browser and this page to turn it off:

https://appleid.apple.com/account/manage

The next time you try to log into the Apple website or an Apple device like an iPhone, iPad, computer or Apple TV, you'll get a special code delivered to one of your other devices.

You'll have to enter this code to allow the login to proceed.

It's a tiny bit more work to log in, but the extra protection is worth it. Trust me.

27

Create a medical ID for emergencies

While you're probably familiar with the concept of an ICE contact, that is, someone listed in your address book to call In Case of Emergency, today's smartphones go way beyond this basic functionality.

In fact, if your phone is locked, someone who is trying to help you in an emergency wouldn't be able to access your ICE contact anyway.

That is, unless you set up the iPhone to properly handle your emergency information.

It only takes a few minutes to set up but this could be the most important chapter you ever read.

iPhone lets you set a **Medical ID** full of vital information about you that could come in handy in a life-threatening situation.

The best part about it is that anyone can access this information on your phone without having to unlock it first.

Now, you might be wondering, is a paramedic or first responder really going to check my pocket first for a phone when I'm unconscious so they can see my blood type and call my emergency contact? Perhaps not, but I was reading an interesting thread on the website Reddit that polled emergency folks on the issue and the consensus seemed to be that it's more helpful to have it than to not have it.

First responders want to stabilize you as fast as possible – while they probably don't have time to take a deep dive into this information, folks at the hospital might find it useful later on. It can also come in handy in a wide variety of other situations, so it's probably best to have it set up. You just never know how it could help.

To set it up, go into the **Health** app – you know, the one with the heart icon on it.

In the row of options at the bottom, tap on the section labeled **Medical ID**. From here, tap "Create Medical ID." If you've previously set up this feature, you can use the **Edit** button in the upper right-hand corner to add or remove information.

Cancel   **Medical ID**   Done

EMERGENCY ACCESS

Show When Locked

Your Medical ID can be viewed when iPhone is locked by tapping Emergency, then Medical ID. On Apple Watch, press and hold the side button and drag the Medical ID slider to the right.

This information is not included in your Health Data or shared with other apps.

 Rich DeMuro

⊕ add date of birth

Medical Conditions
None listed

Medical Notes
None listed

Allergies & Reactions
None listed

Medications
None listed

Take the time to set up your Medical ID

From the edit screen, you will see a bunch of options starting with "Show When Locked." Before you begin, make sure this is toggled on. This way anyone who has your phone can see the information you enter here without unlocking it first.

It's a good idea to keep this in mind as you fill out the information – you probably don't want to include your Social Security Number or ATM PIN number. Just keep in mind that this information is easily accessible to anyone with your phone in their hand.

Now get to editing! You might notice that certain items are already filled out, like your profile photo, name and date of birth.

You can change any of this by tapping on the data and editing the information. If you don't want a section at all then you can tap the icon that looks like a circle with a red line through it and confirm by hitting the Delete option that appears.

The screen gives you the option to add Medical Conditions, Medical Notes, Allergies & Reactions, Medications, as well as blood type, organ donor, Weight and Height. You can be as elaborate as you like, filling out just the sections that apply to you.

The most important section here might be EMERGENCY CONTACTS. You'll want to add at least one person who you can rely on in an emergency situation. Tap the plus sign next to "add emergency contact" and you'll see your familiar address book pop up.

First, select a name and optionally a phone number if they have more than one listed, then you'll see a screen to choose their Relationship to you. There's a laundry list including mother, father, parent, spouse, partner, assistant, roommate, doctor and simply emergency. You can add several entries if you'd like. Repeat the process until you are happy with your list.

These EMERGENCY CONTACTS have two functions – first, someone will be able to dial their phone number from your phone's lock screen without entering your password. I'll show you how that works in a moment. But this list of contacts will also get a text message if you ever use the Emergency SOS function on iPhone or Apple Watch.

You can activate this feature (once it's turned on) by pressing the side button five times fast. Your iPhone will dial the appropriate emergency phone number for your location – if you're in the United States, it would be 911. Additionally, these contacts will get a text message with your current location every 10 minutes for 24 hours or until you cancel.

When you're finished entering your medical information and selecting your contacts, be sure to hit the Done button at the top of the screen in the upper right-hand corner to save your work.

Now let's see how to access this information from the lock screen. Make sure your phone is locked then swipe or press the home button to bring up your Passcode screen – the one that shows a bunch of numbers so you can type in your Passcode.

Don't type anything in, but look at the bottom of the screen for the word Emergency and tap it. Notice how the screen changes to white and there is an emergency dialer that allows you to call an emergency phone number. Look at the bottom of this screen for Medical ID and tap there.

Immediately, you'll get a Medical ID screen with all of the

information you just typed into the Health app. It will list all of your pertinent details including the EMERGENCY CONTACTS you specified. From here on out, anyone will be able to access this screen to see your information and/or tap on one of these contacts to make a call to them without having to unlock your phone.

If there's something you entered in the Health app that you see on the Medical ID screen that you're not comfortable potentially sharing with anyone who finds your phone, then you can go back in and edit your information.

Now that you know how to do this, help a friend set theirs up. It just might save a life.

28

Send an Emergency SOS

If you're ever in an emergency situation, your iPhone can help you dial for help fast – even if you don't know the number for emergency services where you are.

Sure, we know it's 911 here in the United States, but what if you're in Italy, Japan or Greece?

iPhone can help you summon assistance instantly with a feature called Emergency SOS.

You just have to make sure the feature is turned on and be familiar with how it works.

Emergency SOS works in various countries around the world by dialing the local emergency number for that region. In some cases, you might be presented with a secondary screen that asks you to clarify medical or police help.

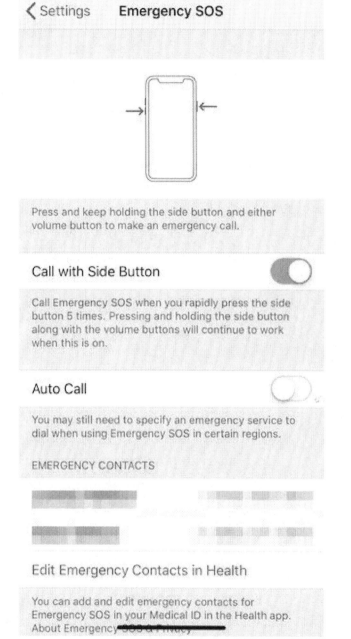

Emergency SOS can be a life saver

To set up the feature, go into **Settings > Emergency SOS**. Make sure the option for "Call with Side Button" is turned on.

Now, when you press the side button on your phone 5 times fast, your phone will go into an emergency mode.

Your next choice is to decide if your device will automatically dial for help, or wait for you to confirm your decision.

This is labeled Auto Call.

If you turn this on, you won't have to take an additional step for the phone call to be dialed.

Let me explain both options. If you press your side button five times with Auto Call enabled, your phone will immediately go into SOS mode. You'll hear a siren sound and see a visual countdown until the phone starts dialing emergency services. You will an option to stop the iPhone from dialing, but you better be quick!

If you press the side button five times with Auto Call turned off, your phone will show you a screen with an Emergency SOS slider.

You will have to manually drag the slide to dial emergency services, like 911.

If you want the least friction between you and dialing, you should leave Auto Call enabled. Just keep in mind your phone will dial 911 or the local emergency number fast!

Two more things to know about using the Emergency SOS option.

First, when your call is completed, your iPhone will send a text to your Emergency contacts with your current location, unless you choose to cancel this. Your contacts will get an update if your location changes. This will happen for 24 hours. You will see a banner at the top of your screen to

Stop Sharing Emergency Location. You can tap there at any time to stop sending updates to your Emergency Contacts.

If you haven't set them up, look for the tip on Creating a Medical ID.

Also, once you activate Emergency SOS, you won't be able to unlock your phone using Face ID or your fingerprint the next time you try. Your phone will require your passcode for an added layer of security.

29

See which apps can access your location

Now, more than ever, there is a heightened interest in the privacy of our personal information and the data our phones are handing over to the products, services, and apps we use.

The good news is that as far as smartphone platforms go, the iPhone and Apple actually do a pretty good job of keeping your data as private as possible unless you want to share it.

Specifically, apps in iOS are generally sandboxed so they can't necessarily gain access to information unless you grant them permission.

But it can happen. We all heard about the story of the Flashlight app that was secretly collecting GPS data on everyone who used it.

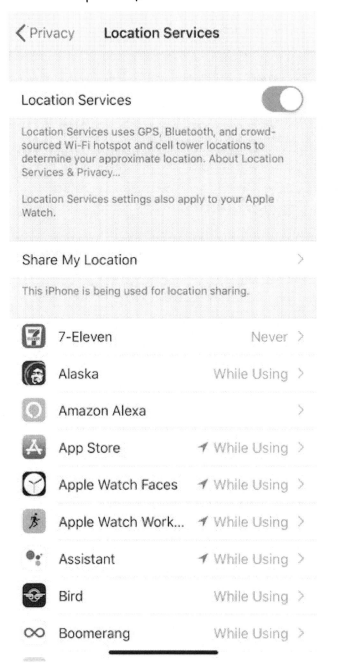

Decide which apps get to access your location

Here's a quick and easy way to do a privacy checkup on your iPhone to make sure no one has access to more information than they need to.

Go to **Settings** > **Privacy** to access a list of all of your phone's sensors. You'll see **Location Services, Contacts, Calendars, Reminders, Photos and more**.

These are all of the shared items and data on your phone that apps can request access to. You've seen the screens before – they usually appear when you load an app for the first time. These permission granting windows also appear when you use a new function on an app for the first time, such as uploading a photo or using the mic.

An app will ask for permission to use your Location, Microphone, Photos, Camera and more. Many times, there's not much of a choice – for instance, if you say no to a maps app when it wants to use your Location, you're not going to get very far with it.

Likewise, if you say no to a photo sharing app that wants access to your Camera Roll, good luck trying to upload a picture.

Apple lets app developers write in a little line about why they are requesting the permissions they are asking for. For instance, Waze might say it needs access to the Microphone so you can use voice commands to control the app.

Granting these permissions is ultimately up to you. When in doubt, just say no.

For instance, if you don't see yourself using voice controls inside Waze, just say no. The app will still load and work properly, you just won't be able to tap the microphone to use voice commands. If you do tap the mic, the app will just ask you to grant the permission.

Now that you have a good idea of what these permissions are all about, let's take a look at each category and see what we've said yes to in the past and figure out if now is the time to revoke those permissions for a more secure mobile experience.

Again, looking in **Settings** > **Privacy**, we see the first section: **Location Services**.

This is an easy one. Tap **Location Services** to bring up a list of all of the apps on your phone and see what type of access they have to your location.

Usually, it's one of three types – Never, While Using the App and Always. Look through your list of apps and figure out what makes sense for each situation.

For instance, the 7-Eleven app on my phone has "Never" listed next to it. If I tap Never, I can see my other option including While Using the App and Always. Under the option, I see the app developer's explanation as to why they want location access on my phone.

In the case of 7-Eleven, it says that "This helps us provide awesome custom offers, products and services while you're in our stores. Fair enough, but I'll take my chances and pay a little more for my coffee, even if it means missing out on an "awesome custom offer."

Go through each app and decide what level of location access it needs. Keep in mind, you can't break anything here. If you take away access that an app needs to function properly or like it did before you tweaked these settings, the app will just ask you again for permission the next time you open it or use the feature that requires the permission.

At the very least, scan the list for any app that has "Always" listed next to it to be sure that it's an app that truly needs your location information 24/7.

Back out of Location Services and tap on the next item in the list – **Contacts**.

Here, you'll see a different type of screen – there are no options, just toggle switches. Green means you've given that app permission to see all of the contacts on your phone. You can tap one of the toggles to turn off access – keep in mind this does not delete any data the app already took from your phone. It just won't get any new data moving forward.

Backing out of Contacts, you can now go down the list. **Calendars** and **Reminders** have similar toggle switches.

Tap to open **Photos** and you'll see a list of apps that want access to your Photos, along with some new options – Read and Write, Never or Add Photos Only.

Be particularly careful with Photos, since they can contain a lot of sensitive information, including the GPS location where they were taken.

You can go through and revoke access to any app you don't think needs to look at your pictures.

Microphone is another important section. I know a lot of conspiracy theorists believe that Facebook is listening into your microphone (they aren't) but if you can't shake that suspicion, just revoke access. Keep in mind you won't be able to use microphone related functions of the app unless you grant access again.

Repeat the process for the other items in the Privacy list, including Camera, Health and others. As more apps pop up to help us with well being, it will become increasingly important to monitor which apps have permission to data in the Motion & Fitness category. This can reveal a lot about your health.

Scroll all the way to the bottom of the screen to reveal two more "system" categories in Privacy. They are **Analytics and Advertising**.

Analytics deals with how you use your phone and accessories. If you leave the option labeled **Share iPhone & Watch Analytics** on, it's a way for Apple to improve their products and see how people use them. This is a personal preference. Your phone won't function any differently if you turn it off.

Same goes for **Share iCloud Analytics**. If you leave these on, which most people likely do, you're helping Apple collect a ton of data from its products so it can figure out issues, improvements and even the features no one ever uses.

Advertising is also a personal preference. There are two options here – **Limit Ad Tracking** and **Reset Advertising Identifier**. Limit Ad Tracking means that marketing companies won't have a solid way of identifying you when you use an app or visit a website. Keep in mind I said "solid way" – they still have their ways. That's why they call the option "limit" and not "stop."

If you choose to Reset Advertising Identifier, you'll generate a new code that identifies you to marketing agencies. Think of this as a fresh profile – it might take them some time to re-associate all of the things they know about you with this new code.

Thanks to Apple's new push in trying to be a bit more transparent about the data they collect on you, you can now tap "View Ad Information" to see the information Apple uses to target advertising to your account. It's pretty interesting, and some of it might be correct, other data might be a bit off. It's always eye-opening to see, though.

Now that you've gone through some of these privacy settings, give yourself a pat on the back!

Then, tear that tin foil off of your windows and take a deep breath. Don't you feel better???

30

Make Face ID more secure

Face ID is Apple's successor to the fingerprint scan, and it's here to stay.

Whether you're on your first or second device with the feature, here is a way to make it a bit more secure.

Although Apple has gone to great lengths to make Face ID both convenient and safe, you can make it harder for someone to use your face to unlock your phone without your permission.

By this, I mean by holding your phone in front of your face to unlock it.

Apple realizes that there might be a circumstance where someone, like your kid, holds your phone up in front of your face to unlock it or authorize an app purchase.

< Settings   **Face ID & Passcode**

ATTENTION

Require Attention for Face ID

TrueDepth camera will provide an additional level of
security by verifying that you are looking at iPhone
before unlocking. Some sunglasses may block attention
detection.

Attention Aware Features

TrueDepth camera will check for attention before
dimming the display or lowering the volume of alerts.

Turn Passcode Off

Change Passcode

Require Passcode   Immediately >

Make Face ID more secure with this setting on

That's why there's a feature called **Require Attention for Face ID**.

Basically, this means that your eyes must be focused on the screen of the iPhone for it to unlock. It needs to see more than just your face, it wants to know that you are actively looking at your phone to unlock it.

I recommend turning this feature on for an extra level of security.

You can find it in **Settings > Face ID & Passcode** under the section labeled ATTENTION. Make sure the toggle next to Require Attention for Face ID is turned on.

Now, try it out.

Lock your phone, then bring it near your face but don't look directly at the screen. Sort of turn your head and gaze off to the side. Then swipe to unlock your phone. It won't unlock. Now, bring your face center and look at the screen and you should notice it unlock immediately.

Even though it recognizes your face from the slight angle, it knows you are not looking at the screen and that's why it stays locked.

You can try this again by locking your phone and closing your eyes and swiping up to unlock and access your home screen. With Require Attention for Face ID turned on, your phone won't unlock until you open your eyes. Pretty neat, right?

Alternatively, if you have a physical condition that prohibits you from being able to focus your eyes on your phone screen, you'll want to turn the Require Attention for Face ID toggle off. This way you can easily unlock your phone with no issues.

31

———

Share your location with family members

There is a fast and easy way to keep tabs on the locations of all of your family members and friends using iPhones or iOS devices. It's all thanks to an app called Find My Friends. It's built right into your phone, all you have to do is set it up and you can see the location of your friends on a map.

To start, just open the **Find My Friends** app. If it's not installed for some reason, just install it from the App Store. You might have to Allow access to your location the first time you open the app.

Immediately, you will see your own location on a map. Before we add some friends or family members, let's take a look at our information.

Tap the bottom of the screen where it says Me. You'll see the address of your current location. If it's a place you frequent, like your home or work, you can label it by taping the area that says Label. You can choose from seem pre-populated labels like Work, School and Gym, or add your own.

On this screen you'll also see the option to Share My Location, you can toggle this at any time to turn off the sharing of your location.

You'll also see a list of devices you can share your location from. You can choose the one you use the most if you have multiple devices listed.

Under invitations, you can select which email address your invitations will be sent from in case you have multiple emails linked to your Apple ID.

Hit done to exit your profile screen and let's add some friends.

The way this works is that you have to share your location with someone in order for them to share theirs with you. It's sort of a two-way street.

For starters, hit the Add button in the upper right-hand corner and type in the name, email address or phone number of one of your contacts. Keep in mind they must be using Find My Friends on their devices for this to work.

They'll get a request to share their location. Once they accept, you'll be able to see them on your map for a certain period of time that they specify. If you're setting this up for family members, you'll probably want to choose the Indefinitely option.

If you want to remove someone from your list and map, just

swipe left on their name and hit the Trash Can button that appears. I know, how harsh is that?

There are some other options built into this location sharing. Let's say you're leaving a friends house late at night and they want to be sure you arrive safely at home. Tap the name of the person you want to be notified, then towards the top center of the screen hit the Notify button. You can now specify that they get a notification when you leave or arrive at a certain area.

You can even set this to repeat every time.

One example of this would be if your child has an iPhone and you want an alert every day when they arrive at school, leave school or arrive home. You can go to their Find My Friends app and set up a notification so you will be sent a recurring alert every time this happens. This can also be useful for when your partner leaves work each day. You can get an alert so you have a rough estimate of when they might arrive home.

A few other things to note about the Find My Friends feature. You can have up to 100 friends in the app and you don't really need to worry about this feature draining your battery. Your phone's location is only sent when your friends request it – that is, open the app on their phone or send a new request.

32

See the secret location data your phone is collecting

This one might surprise you.

Your iPhone isn't spying on you, but it is keeping a list of the places you frequent the most.

There are reasons for this. Siri wants to know where you go the most so it can recommend when to leave for appointments, help you out when putting items in your calendar, tagging photos and more.

While it's important to know that a list of these frequent locations exists on every iPhone, it can also be helpful to know how to clear them out if you ever find yourself wanting to do a digital cleanse.

I'm not telling you this to scare you or help you catch a cheating spouse, but I'm telling you this because it's your information, and you should be in the driver's seat anytime a device is collecting this kind of highly personal data on you.

For what it's worth, Apple says that all of these locations are stored encrypted and not seen by the company.

Now, let's take a look.

You're going to have to dig a bit to reveal these locations.

Go to **Settings** > **Privacy** > **Location Services** > **System Services** (scroll all the way to the bottom!) > **Significant Locations**.

Since we're accessing some sensitive data here, you'll need to unlock the final screen with your fingerprint, Face ID or passcode.

Once you do, you will see a list labeled HISTORY with what your iPhone considers Significant Locations.

You might see a bunch of places you frequent – like work, home or the gym – but there could also be others that you don't consider significant.

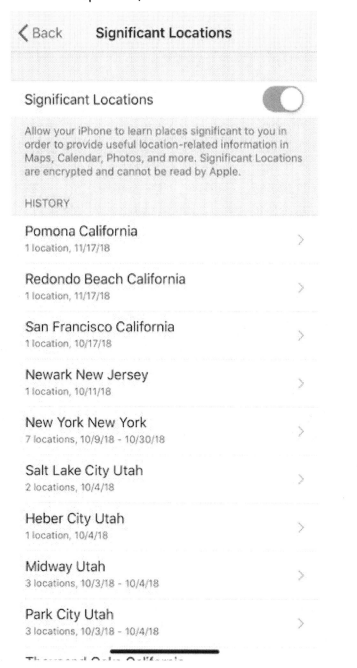

Oh, the places you've gone

I'm seeing a bunch of places I frequent, as well as places that I've visited just once or twice. What you see will depend on how long you've had your phone and where you've taken it.

When you tap a city, you can see a list of the places you visited there.

Some might be just an address, others might be a specific business name.

For some places, you'll see even more information, like a list of how many times you visited a particular location.

For some of you, this might be a trip down memory lane. Others will want to know how to get rid of all of this information – or even stop its collection – immediately. You can do that too.

If you want to delete one particular location, drill down to that location and swipe left on it to bring up a DELETE button. Keep in mind this only works for individual locations, not when they are grouped by city.

If you back to the main Significant Locations screen – the one with the section labeled HISTORY – you can scroll all the way down to the bottom of the list and see a button labeled Clear History.

You can tap here to reset your Significant Locations on both this device and across any other devices signed into the same iCloud account.

You can also stop the collection of Significant Locations entirely. Go back up to the top of the Significant Locations settings page and you'll see a toggle switch. If you turn it off, your iPhone will stop monitoring where you go.

How will this impact your iPhone experience? It will make your phone a bit less smart when it comes to predicting things.

For example, let's say you are headed home after work and open Maps. Usually, your phone uses Significant Locations to understand that you are probably headed home since this is the time you usually leave the office.

It will offer up a travel report with an estimated time to your destination, or even help you avoid traffic if there is a major accident.

With significant locations turned off, your phone won't be able to do these things. That's just one example of how it can impact your overall iPhone experience, but there are more.

I didn't show you this to scare you or make you turn this feature off, I just think it's important to know where stuff like this is, especially when it's incredibly personal and private.

PART IV

Fun Tricks

33

Turn your iPhone into a magnifying glass

Turning your iPhone into a magnifying glass is one of the most popular tips I've ever shared, and it is pretty much the inspiration for this book.

Turns out people were very happy to find out that they could finally see a restaurant menu without their glasses or a physical magnifying glass. True story: my father in law used to carry a credit card sized magnifying sheet in his wallet, but not since I showed him this!

There is a magnifier function built into the iPhone, you just have to know where to find it and how to activate it. It's pretty simple, and all it takes is a one-time setup.

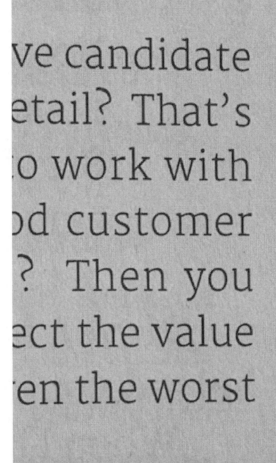

Yep, your iPhone is a magnifying glass too

After that, you can use your iPhone camera lens as sort of a virtual magnifying glass!

First, go into **Settings** > **General** > **Accessibility** and look for the option labeled "Magnifier."

Tap it so you can see the toggle to turn it on.

Let's try it out: exit out of this screen completely and lock your phone.

Now, **triple click your iPhone's side button**. If you have an iPhone with a home button, triple click it fast. No matter which phone you have, these actions are quick, deliberate and in fast succession. If you click too slow, you'll just turn your phone screen on and off or bring up Apple Pay.

Done right, your phone will immediately spring into Magnifier mode!

Now, hold your iPhone over some small text, then use the slider below the screen to zoom in and make the text bigger!

There are some additional controls you can take advantage of.

The lightning bolt icon will turn on a flash.

Tap the Lock icon to "freeze" the focus and turn off autofocus.

The shutter button will let you take a still image of the item you're magnifying. You can then use the slider to zoom in or move around the image like you would a picture.

The icon with the three overlapping circles will allow you to add filters to your magnifying glass that might make it easier for you to see and read, depending on your particular preferences.

Keep in mind, if you choose a filter, these settings will "stick" the next time you use the magnifier. If you don't want any filters applied, be sure to select the NONE option before you exit the filters screen.

One more thing to know – once the feature is turned on in settings, you can activate the magnifier from anywhere. Your phone screen can be on or off.

Remember, to bring up magnifier just click the side button or home button three times fast to bring it up.

You'll never look at menus the same way again. Literally.

34

———

Clear all notifications at once

Notifications have gotten a lot better in iOS 12, now that they can be grouped by app, but they can still get a bit unwieldy on the iPhone.

Here's the fastest way I know to obliterate all of them instantly.

But before we get to this blazing fast method of removing all traces of your notifications at once, let me show you a few ways to access them.

For starters, if your phone is just laying on a table and the screen is off, you can double tap the screen or hit the home button to wake it up.

If you have a recent notification or two, you will see them here.

But wait, there's more!

Try swiping up from the center of your screen to reveal even more notifications!

I call this the notification graveyard.

Apple groups and hides older notifications by default in an effort to clean up your lock screen a bit. Now, you know where to find these lingering notifications.

You're probably used to tapping on a notification to bring you into the app, but there are many more commands available.

Swipe left to right on a notification to bring up some new choices to help you deal with them.

All the way on the right you'll see an option labeled **Clear** or **Clear All**, depending if this notification is part of a group of notifications from the same app. A tap of this will clear out the notification or all of them in that group.

To the left of that is **View**. Tap it to view the notification in its entirety.

If you want a notification to take you into the app that generated it, just swipe right on the notification. You'll reveal an **Open** command. Keep swiping to perform the open action.

Clear all of your notifications fast with 3D Touch

Now, the other way to access your entire list of notifications is to swipe down from the top of the screen when your phone is unlocked. You can be on your home screen or inside any app and this will work. Just pull down on the screen by dragging from the left-hand corner of your phone where it says the name of your wireless carrier like AT&T, Verizon, etc.

This will bring up a list of all of your notifications. Notice how they're in groups? You might see sections labeled Earlier Today, Yesterday or even earlier days of the week.

Look for the X in a circle at the top of each group of notifications.

Try tapping that X so it turns into the world **Clear**. Tap the word Clear and watch all of the notifications in that section disappear instantly.

But here is the really fun part.

Instead of tapping that X in the circle, 3D Touch it.

You should see a new, bigger button appear that says **Clear All Notifications**.

Tap here and it will clear out all of your notifications instantly.

Talk about a fresh start! Doing this always feels so good to me – it's incredibly satisfying to get rid of all of these nagging messages at once.

35

Make your LED flash for notifications

Want more than just a sound notification when your phone rings or you get a message?

You can use a feature on the iPhone that will flash the LED with a quick burst of light to get your attention (and possibly the attention of everyone around you).

This functionality is intended as an accessibility feature for those with hearing or other issues, but lots of people like turning it on since there's less of a chance of a missed call or notification.

It can come in handy if you work in a loud setting or are anywhere you might not hear your phone ringing or feel it vibrating.

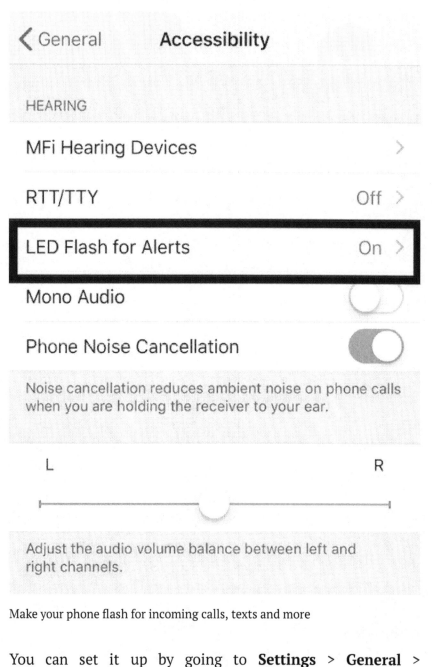

Make your phone flash for incoming calls, texts and more

You can set it up by going to **Settings** > **General** > **Accessibility**. Look for the section labeled HEARING.

In here, you will see an option labeled "LED Flash for Alerts." Tap to see your options and turn it on.

Once you do, you'll see a secondary option appear called Flash on Silent.

If you turn on this option, your phone will flash even if silent mode is enabled. If you keep it off, your phone will stay silent in all ways – visual and audible – when you have your ringer set to silent mode.

Now, try calling your phone and watch it light up!

36

Change the flashlight brightness

The flashlight on the iPhone can be a lifesaver. It can light up a dark night, help you find something deep in the recesses of your bag or check for an issue in your kid's mouth. (Yeah, been there.)

It's a simple tool that we've all come to rely on. Tap the flashlight icon to turn it on, another tap turns it off. Doesn't get much easier than that.

But there's more to it than just a tap.

You can actually adjust the intensity of the iPhone flashlight!

Before I explain how, let me run through the various ways to activate the flashlight on the iPhone.

The latest way is to use the flashlight icon on the lock screen. It's in the lower left-hand corner. You'll notice that a tap isn't sufficient enough to toggle it on – you'll need to give it a firm press. This is to keep you from mistakenly activating the flashlight in your pocket.

And yes, I've seen plenty of people walking around with their iPhone flashlight still on in their pocket. Look, it happens. They'll figure it out when their phone gets hot enough, or they walk past a mirror and see a little light shining through the fabric of their pants. (Yeah, been there, too.)

Another firm press will turn the flashlight off from the lock screen.

You can also access the flashlight from the Control Center.

Once you open it up, you will see the same flashlight icon that's on your lock screen.

From here, one tap will turn the light on or off.

But here is where the fun part comes in. You can actually adjust the brightness level of your flashlight with a 3D Touch of the icon in Control Center.

3D Touch the icon and that will bring up an entirely new flashlight intensity slider!

Adjust the flashlight intensity with 3D Touch

You now have access to five levels of LED brightness – the first is completely off, next is 25% brightness, 50% brightness, 75% brightness and 100% brightness.

Go ahead, slide it up and down and watch the beam adjust. Just don't do what I just did and look directly into the light as you adjust it (and yes, I did the same thing writing the second version of this book!) Now I'm seeing iPhone flashlight silhouettes all over my computer screen.

Once you've adjusted the slider to your liking, you can exit it by tapping anywhere on the screen except on the slider itself.

A few notes here – whatever you set the intensity at "sticks" for the next time you activate the flashlight. So if you activate the flashlight, and then adjust it down to 50%, the next time you turn on the flashlight it will fire up at 50%.

The exception to this is if you turn the slider all the way down so the flashlight goes off, and then you tap on the screen to exit the slider. The next time you tap the flashlight app to turn it on the flashlight will fire at 25%, or the dimmest setting possible.

The next time you want to use your flashlight to illuminate a menu in a dimly lit restaurant, you can fire up at just 25% brightness! This will prove to be a bit more subtle but still give you the light you need to read the text.

Once you've ordered, show your friends your newfound iPhone trick. Then let them know there are 100 more in my book.

Many thanks in advance.

37

Tap the time to go back to the top

Ever scroll so far down on a page that you dread trying to get back to the top?

Yeah, didn't think so... but it was worth a try!

Still, there are times when you want to jump back to the top of a page you've scrolled down on. Here is the fast and easy way to accomplish that without actually scrolling back up!

Next time, all you have to do is tap the time. Invariably, this will take you right back to the top of a page, whether it's inside an app or on the web.

Try it. Navigate to a website – preferably a long article – and scroll all the way down the screen, or until your finger gets tired, whichever happens first.

6:56 ⌁

richontech.tv

Prior to joining KTLA, Rich was a
Senior Editor at the technology
website CNET and worked as a
reporter at Channel One News and
local TV stations in Yakima,
Washington and Shreveport,
Louisiana.

Rich is originally from New Jersey
and graduated from the University of
Southern California with a degree in
Broadcast Journalism. He lives in Los
Angeles with his wife and sons and
enjoys traveling, reading, running,
magic, movies, music and writing.

You can watch Rich's "Tech Smart"

Tap the time to return to the top of a page

Now, tap the time at the top of the screen.

You should be instantly taken back to the top of the page. This feature works in many of Apple's default apps, as well as various other apps that have enabled the shortcut. It might not work in every app, but more often than not, it should.

Now that you've gone to the top, perhaps you would like to go back to the bottom. As it turns out, that functionality isn't built into the iPhone, or at least I haven't found it.

Well, there is one exception to the rule in the Photos app.

You can get back to the "bottom" of the screen, or in this case, catch up to the last photo in your camera roll.

Once you've done some scrolling in your camera roll, just tap the Photos tab at the bottom of the screen a few times. This will take you right back to your most recent picture.

38

Fit more icons in your dock

Think fast: how many apps can you fit in the little dock at the bottom of your iPhone's home screen?

If you answered four, you're wrong!

You can actually fit more with this trick.

If you're not familiar with the concept of the dock, this is the lower portion of your iPhone's home screen that stays the same no matter which secondary home screen you swipe to. There is also a faint background behind the four apps.

You'll notice it's also located under a few dots. Each dot represents one of the iPhone home screens you can swipe between. I'll wait while you swipe between them and count them off.

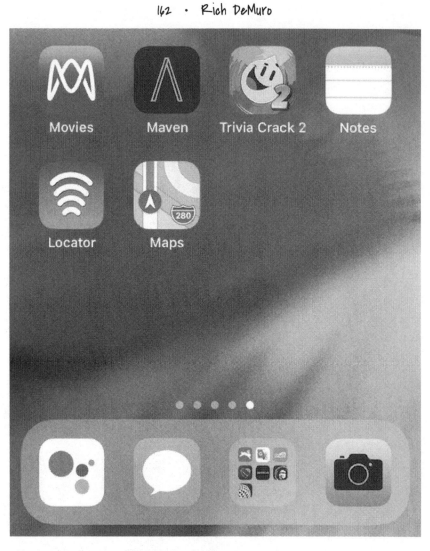

Fit more icons in your dock with a folder

Ok, we're back.

Usually, you can only drag four app icons into the dock. If you try to drag another icon on top of an app that's already there to create a folder like you normally would on a home screen, nothing happens.

But, if you create a folder first and then drag it into the dock it stays there just fine!

Try it – drag one of the apps in your dock out of the dock and onto your home screen to leave space for a new app.

Now, instead of dragging another app into the unoccupied space, try dragging an entire folder in there. You'll see that it sits there just fine. Tap it and it will expand as normal so you can access all the apps inside.

The main difference between a folder that sits in your dock versus a folder on your home screen is that you won't be able to see the name of the folder under it. However, a tap will reveal both the folder contents and the name of the folder.

There you go. More apps on the dock. Especially handy if you want one home screen to rule them all.

39

Reveal the hidden search bar in settings

The Settings section of the iPhone has really expanded in recent years. There are so many options to go through. If you're a super nerd like me, one of my favorite things to do on a Friday night is to go through every single one of these options, explore their functionality and choose the best settings for me.

You're probably NOT like me, so I'm assuming you just want to find the setting you need to change in the fastest way possible, adjust it and get on with your life. That's OK, too.

This tip is so simple it amazes me how hidden it is to so many people:

Pull down on the Settings screen to reveal a search bar.

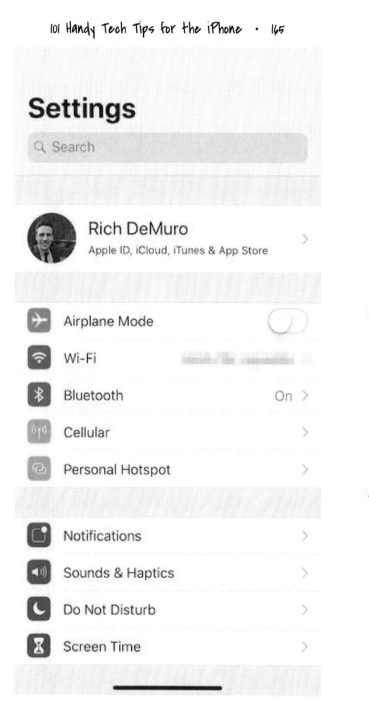

Pull down on the Settings screen to reveal a search bar

Yep, you can go into Settings and just drag down on the screen.

Amazingly, a little search bar will appear under the Settings header and above your ID information.

Now, you can jump straight into a Settings section just by searching for it in the box.

Want to change your Wallpaper? Type Wallpaper.

Want Bold Text? Type Text.

Change your Ringtone? Type Ring.

You get the idea.

Apple doesn't really give you any hints on what to search in here, and most searches have to match one of the features on the phone.

But again, if you're a nerd like me you'll start typing A and see what comes up. (Airplane Mode, Manage Account, Choose a Data Plan)

B is for Backup, Bluetooth, Auto-Brightness and Background App Refresh.

C is for iCloud, Contacts, Calendar and iCloud Drive.

Clearly, I've been reading too many children's books to my kids at bedtime.

This is one of the most powerful tools for changing the settings on your iPhone even when you're not sure if they exist.

Need to do something with WiFi, Privacy or Safari? Just search in Settings and chances are, you'll find what you need.

40

Have your phone say who's calling out loud

If your phone always seems to ring at the most inconvenient times – like when your hands are full or you just walked into another room without it – you'll love this tip.

You can have your iPhone announce who's calling out loud so you always know if you need to answer!

If the caller is in your address book, your iPhone will actually say their name before your phone rings – if they're not in your address book, your iPhone will say unknown caller.

To turn on the feature, go to **Settings** > **Phone**. Look for the feature labeled "Announce Calls."

Tap and you'll get four options: **Always, Headphones & Car, Headphones Only** and **Never**.

< Settings   **Phone**

My Number   ▪ ▪▪▪ ▪▪▪ ▪▪▪▪

CALLS

Announce Calls   Always >

Call Blocking & Identification   >

SMS/Call Reporting   >

Wi-Fi Calling   Off >

Calls on Other Devices   Off >

Respond with Text   >

Change Voicemail Password

Dial Assist   ⬤━

Dial assist automatically determines the correct
international or local prefix when dialing.

Have Siri say the name of your callers

Always will have Siri read you the name of your caller when your phone rings – assuming it's not set to silent.

Headphones & Car will have Siri read you the name of your caller when you have headphones connected or you are in your car.

Headphones Only will have Siri read you the name of your caller when you have headphones connected – this can be handy if your phone is in your pocket. You can hear who's calling without taking your phone out, as long as the person is in your contacts.

Never is sort of self-explanatory and probably the setting you had enabled up until now.

Choose your preferred announcement setting, then have a friend call you. You'll hear a friendly Siri announce your friend's name before your phone rings. I think it would be nice if Siri said the person's name between each ring or the digits of unknown callers, but Apple hasn't given us these options yet.

Still, Announce Calls can be especially useful if you're always on the go with your iPhone in a bag, pocket or tucked safely away from distraction while you drive.

Personally, since writing this tip I've left this feature on and I find that it's really nice to have on even at home – now you know who's calling even when your phone is across the room.

41

The secret way to erase one calculator digit

Go ahead and open up the Calculator app on the iPhone.

Now, find the delete key.

It's not there, right?

While it might seem like Apple made a glaring omission, there actually is a delete function, you just have to know the proper gesture to accomplish it.

All it takes is a swipe!

Swipe left or right on digits to erase them one by one

To prove it, just type in some numbers on the calculator.

Now, let's say you made a mistake. In the past, you would probably just hit the C button to start over.

But this time, just swipe left or right on the numbers.

Watch them disappear one by one.

Amazing? Pretty much.

Imagine if this tip saves everyone who uses the calculator on iPhone just a second because they don't have to retype the entire number in again when they type in the wrong number.

Make no mistake, that would add up to a lot of time.

See what I did there?

42

Turn your keyboard into a trackpad

I've been using the iPhone for a decade now and for some reason, I still can't master the whole magnifying bubble to select text. So here's a faster way. Turn your keyboard into a trackpad.

It's a super easy trick but it can come in handy in a variety of situations. Basically, any time you want to move where the cursor is on the screen without a lot of fuss.

Let's say you just typed an entire love letter in the notes app (is that how kids do it these days?) and you're about to send it off to your crush. But you realize you spelled their name wrong in the second paragraph.

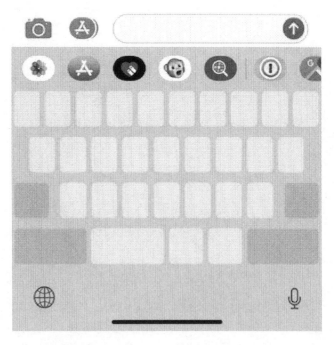

Tap and hold the spacebar to enter trackpad mode

You tap the area where you want to change the word but you end up selecting another word nearby or moving the cursor to a location on the screen you didn't want.

Next time, just **tap and hold on the spacebar to enter trackpad mode**.

When you do, the keys will instantly fade away and you can now move your finger over the keyboard area to move the cursor on the screen like you would a mouse.

Drop the cursor exactly where you need it to be to make a correction or type some new text. It's super fast and easy, and this one also makes a great trick to show your friends. Who knew an old school mouse was built into the iPhone?

43

See when a message was sent

This is one of my all-time favorites when it comes to a super simple, yet useful tip for the iPhone.

It lets you figure out when a message was sent, because, at first glance, the information doesn't seem to be there!

But it is, and just like a lot of hidden iPhone features, you just need to know how to find it.

Here's how to see the exact time a message was sent or received to your phone.

First, go into the **Messages** app and pull up a recent conversation. This trick works equally well on regular texts (green) and iMessages (blue).

Swipe right to left on a message to see its timestamp

You will notice there are some general timestamps if you scroll up and down through messages.

If you want to see the exact time a message was sent or received, all you have to do is swipe.

Put your finger on the chain of messages, then pull on the screen from right to left.

This will reveal a little time stamp to the right of your messages. You can see when you sent a message, along with the time the response came in.

Let go of your screen, and the information goes away.

So remember, the next time you want to see how long it took for someone to respond to your message, or just figure out when it was sent, just tap on a message bubble and swipe to the left.

44

---

uncover the secret redial button

There are so many hidden functions on the iPhone using it is almost like a treasure hunt. The Phone app is no exception.

You've probably dialed numbers hundreds of times, but I bet you never found a redial key. Until now.

First, open the **Phone** app. Then, hit the Keypad option as if you were going to dial a phone number. Now, before you tap any keys, just hit the **Green Phone button**, aka the "start a phone call" button.

See that number pop up on the screen? That is the last number you dialed manually.

Tap the Green Phone icon once more to call it again.

The call button doubles as a top-secret redial button

This would have come in handy for me when I was a teen and I was calling the radio station non-stop to be caller one hundred to win their contests. But back then there was no iPhone and my phone actually had a real redial button, so I guess never mind. I just wanted to share what a nerd I was even back then.

This feature came in handy for me the other day. I was dialing a doctor's office to pay a bill and I got disconnected. Instead of switching to the Recents screen, I simply hit the Green Phone icon to redial the number and I was reconnected in seconds.

How will this newfound knowledge help you?

Only time will tell, but it will save you at least one tap because you don't have to go into the Recents list first to call the phone number you just dialed once again.

At the very least, you might be able to earn a free drink in the bar from your friends if you challenge them to find the redial button on the iPhone.

Bonus points if the number that pops up is yours.

Reconsider your friendship if the number that pops up is your significant other. Just kidding. Well, let's hope that doesn't happen.

45

Delete a number from your recent call list

I'm not trying to help you be sly here, but there might come a time when you don't want a number you called to appear in your Recents list.

Perhaps you dialed the wrong number and don't want to make the same mistake again.

Maybe you just broke up with your significant other and can't bear to see their number anymore.

Whatever the reason, here's the fast and easy way to clear a number out.

First, open the **Phone** app – you know, the one you use to dial calls – and tap the section down below titled Recents.

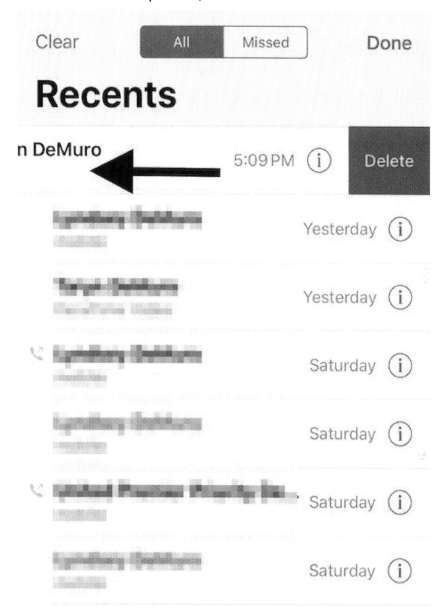

Swipe right to left on a phone number to remove it from your recents list

Now, find the offending entry in the list and swipe from right to left.

This will bring up a **Delete** button. One more tap and the call record is banished from existence.

If you want to do this to multiple calls at once, just tap the Edit button in the upper right-hand corner of your screen.

This will bring up little red circles with a line in the middle. Tap one of them next to a number and you'll see the same red Delete button appear. Tap it to get rid of the call record.

Now, I'm just saying that this method takes 3 taps minimum, 4 if you count the tap to hit the Done button when you're done.

The swipe method takes one swipe and a tap, so it's probably faster for getting rid of entries one by one.

But, if you really find yourself in some sort of Witness Protection Program, you can delete all of these Recents entries at once.

Tap that Edit button once again, then look for the new Clear button that appears in the upper left-hand corner of your screen.

Tap it and you'll get a confirmation button that says **Clear All Recents**. One more tap and all of your recent calls are gone – like you never made them in the first place.

PART V

Take Control

46

Customize your share options

If you've ever shared something on the iPhone, you know that the process can be a little haphazard. This tip will show you how to organize your options so you can share things fast and get rid of the services you might not use or need.

It's one of those things that everyone should do but no one takes the time to do it. But you are different, I know it!

First, let me explain what the "share sheet" is all about since I bet you've never heard it called that before.

The **Share Sheet** is what pops up when you hit the share button in an app. You know, the one that looks like a box with an arrow sticking out of it.

Let's go into the share sheet to organize it.

Tap More to customize your share options

First, open a photo from your **Photos** app, then tap the share button.

You'll see three sections – the top is dedicated to AirDrop, the center lets you share to apps and the bottom row is reserved for system share functions. You can customize the bottom two rows.

Starting with the middle row of apps, you should see a bunch of places you can share photos to.

On my phone, there's Instagram, Message, Twitter, Gmail and more. There are some here that I use often, others I rarely or never use.

To customize the icons you see here, tap the final icon that says **More**.

You will now see a section labeled Activities along with all of the icons we just talked about. Next to many of the icons, you'll see a toggle and grabber icons that look like three lines in a row.

First, let's turn off the apps you don't think you'll need to share to so we can keep our share sheet neat and clean. Just tap the toggle next to the apps you don't see yourself using very much to share items to. Don't worry, you can always turn them back on later.

Now, let's rearrange these icons in the order of the ones we expect to use the most, to the ones we expect to use the least.

You can use those little grabber icons to pick up a row and move it around. You will have to 3D Touch the grabber icons to get them to "pick up." Arrange your rows as you like, then tap Done when you're finished.

This will take you back to the share sheet where you can

admire your handiwork! See those icons, all arranged just as you like, without any extraneous apps? That's your doing!

Next, let's customize the bottom row of the share sheet – this is the section with options including Copy, Slideshow, AirPlay and more. Once again, scroll all the way to the right and tap the More icon.

Here you will notice that there are many fewer apps you can "turn off."

Still, you can rearrange these system functions to your liking using the same grabber icons. For me, I put Use As Wallpaper, Duplicate and Assign to Contact as my top three Activities. Your preferences may vary.

Press **Done** when you're finished.

Voila! Your share sheet is totally customized and streamlined for your specific needs. Isn't that a nice feeling?

But wait, there's more!

Here's one final tip that puts the icing on the cake. Let's say you find yourself using the second icon in the row more than the first. You can actually re-arrange them on the fly, without having to go back into the More menu!

Just tap and hold an icon until it lifts up, and then drag it to a new position in the row, just like you would an app on your home screen. This works both for apps and the system actions on the bottom line. Amazing, right?

One more thing to know. Options on your Share Sheet can be slightly different depending on the app you're accessing it from. Things look a little different when you share from Safari vs Photos. That's OK, you can do the same arranging you just did for that app as well.

47

Quick reply to a notification

Sometimes, a notification arrives on the iPhone but we are so engrossed in what we're doing, we can't stand the idea of leaving the screen we're on to reply.

Next time, try this fast and easy way to reply to messages without interrupting what you're doing.

When a message arrives, instead of tapping it to bring you to the app full screen, just "pull down" on it instead!

This will expand the message but still keep it floating on your screen. This way you won't interrupt the app screen you were on.

You will be able to type your message as normal and send it off.

Pull down or 3D Touch an incoming notification to quick reply

When you're done with your correspondence, you can tap the X in the upper right-hand circle.

Alternatively, you can 3D Touch the incoming message to bring up the same floating reply screen.

Either way, you can chat back and forth as much as you want. When you close out of the window you'll be right back to what you were doing.

This quick reply functionality works with various apps that have enabled it, not just the stock Messages app.

Just keep in mind the pull-down functionality will only work on notifications received while your phone is in use and unlocked. You can use the 3D Touch quick reply method on notifications you get while your phone is in use and those on the lock screen. However, you might have to unlock your phone before you can type a reply.

48

Change your AirDrop preferences fast

AirDrop is an amazingly useful tool built into a wide variety of Apple products including the iPhone, iPad, and computers.

It lets you wirelessly transfer photos, videos, documents and more to a nearby device without connecting them with physical wires or typing in a password to link them together.

It's fast, easy and just sort of works.

There's a lot going on behind the scenes to make this magical transfer work – I'm going to show you a shortcut that will make the setup more secure and help you use the feature more often.

Apple built AirDrop to be simple but also have a level of security.

You've got (AirDrop) options!

Usually, it is set up so you can easily transfer items to nearby people in your address book. The thought is that if you're near a phone and the number of that phone is in your address book, it's likely a trusted person to share with.

However, there might be times when you want to exchange a file with someone that isn't in your address book. AirDrop allows for this as well.

There's also an option to turn off the AirDrop functionality completely.

You can always control your AirDrop status by going to **Settings** > **General** > **AirDrop**.

Here, you can choose from **Receiving Off, Contacts Only** and **Everyone**.

I recommend leaving this setting to Contacts Only. If you don't like the idea of AirDrop, you can turn Receiving Off.

From now on, there is a much easier way to access your AirDrop options to toggle between them.

It's inside the Control Center.

Bring it up, then 3D Touch the box with your wireless controls in it. That's the one with the Airplane, cellular signal, Wifi, and Bluetooth icons.

Once you 3D Touch this area, the box will expand to show more controls including AirDrop!

You can see your current AirDrop setting under the icon. If you want to change it, just tap. Now you can switch to a new option faster than ever.

Now, let's review the AirDrop options.

Receiving Off is the most secure default setting. This way, no one around you can "see" your phone and it's not actively participating in any AirDrop scanning. Ideally, you would always revert to this setting when you're done using AirDrop, but that's sort of tough to remember to do.

So the next best setting is **Contacts Only**.

This means your phone will only let you transfer items with people that are already in your address book in some way.

Everyone is the broadest setting – this means you can

exchange items with anyone around you with an Apple device – whether you know them or not.

With this setting turned on, someone could potentially see the name of your iPhone device and attempt to send you a file. Your iPhone will show you a preview of the file and ask you to accept it.

There have been reported cases where people will send random nearby folks obscene photos via AirDrop. It's probably not common, but you would see a preview of the picture before you hit Decline.

If this makes you uncomfortable, I'd stick to the Contacts Only option.

However, there are times when you might need to use the Everyone setting – like at a business conference or meeting – so just know it's there.

You can toggle between these settings as necessary to exchange files with friends and colleagues.

Just don't forget to turn AirDrop off when you're not using it, or at the very least, default to the Contacts Only setting for security reasons.

49

Adjust your screen for day and night

You've probably noticed your iPhone screen getting brighter or darker depending on its surroundings. Automatic brightness has been a feature for a while now.

But the latest iPhone screens take things a step further and adjust their look to adapt to a variety of lighting conditions and even interfere less with your sleep.

First, let's take a look at something called **True Tone**. This is a relatively new option you'll see when you first set up your iPhone.

It's also the reason why your iPhone screen has a yellowish hue at times.

Apple says the technology uses an ambient light sensor to

adjust the white balance of your screen to match the light around you. The idea is that it results in a better viewing experience.

What this means, in reality, is that your phone screen could look different to you compared to your previous devices.

Phone screens have a tendency of looking super bright white or even a bit blue, but with True Tone turned on the whites on the screen look a bit warmer and almost borderline yellow.

It's a personal preference whether you like the look, but you can toggle True Tone on and off to see which setting you prefer. There are two ways to do it.

You can go into **Settings** > **Display & Brightness** and look for the toggle labeled "True Tone." Turn it on or off and you will notice an immediate impact on the color of your phone's screen.

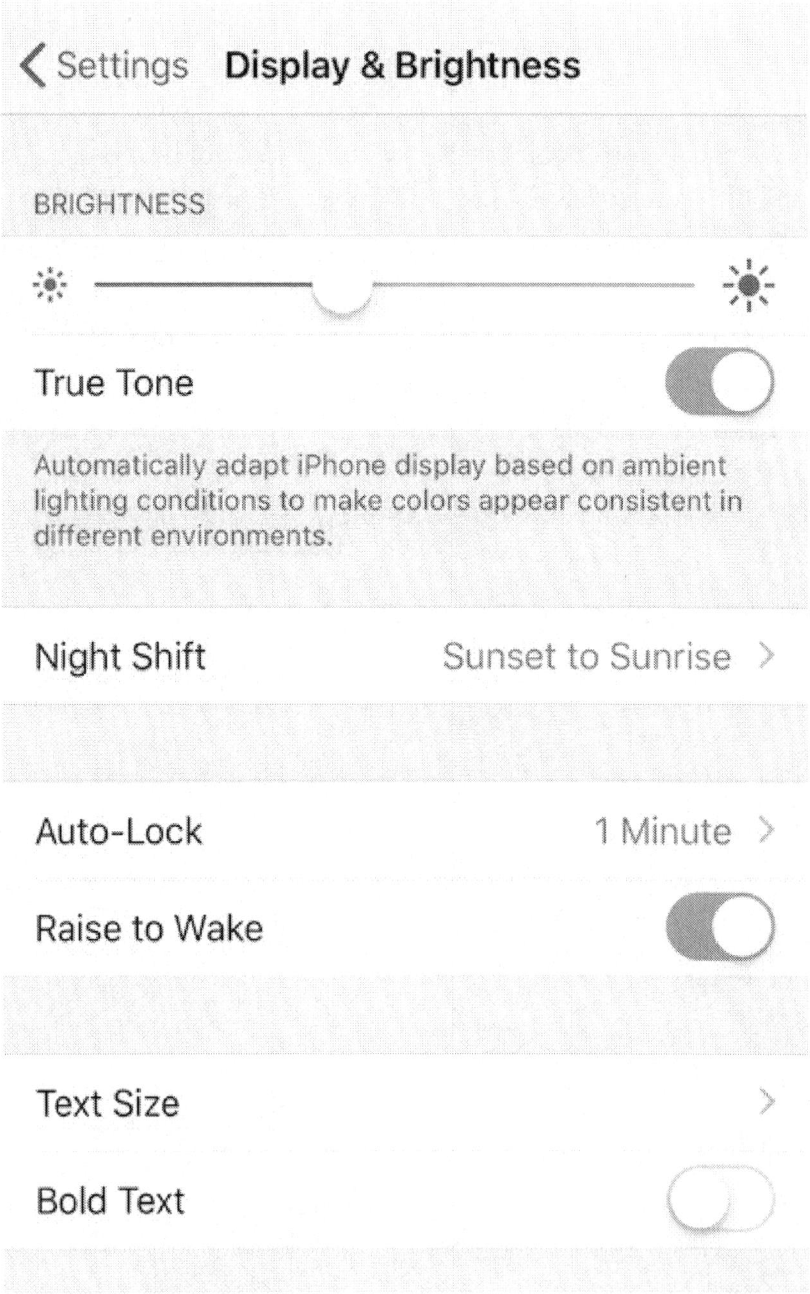

‹ Settings Display & Brightness

BRIGHTNESS

☀ ————————————○————————— ☀

True Tone ⬤

Automatically adapt iPhone display based on ambient lighting conditions to make colors appear consistent in different environments.

Night Shift   Sunset to Sunrise ›

Auto-Lock   1 Minute ›

Raise to Wake ⬤

Text Size   ›

Bold Text ◯

Adjust your screen options so you can sleep better

The other way to toggle True Tone is to go into Control Center and look for the brightness slider. It's the one with the sun logo on it.

3D Touch this slider to bring up more controls, including a True Tone toggle in the lower right-hand corner.

Toggle it and you'll notice the effect it has on the color of your screen.

I find it easier to see the difference when I'm in the settings since so much more of the screen is white. If you are toggling True Tone for the first time I'd go into settings so the difference is more apparent. After that, you can use Control Center to toggle it on and off, if necessary.

The second setting we'll look at is called **Night Shift**. When it's on, blue light is filtered from the screen in an effort to make the screen color warmer and easier on your eyes. Lots of people believe this is helpful for falling asleep and sleeping better since bright blue from electronic screens can trick the brain into thinking it's not bedtime.

Again, this is a personal preference, but I have Night Shift turned on for all of my devices. I can't be sure it helps me sleep but my screens definitely seem easier on the eyes at dusk with it on.

To turn on Night Shift, go into **Settings > Display & Brightness** and look for "Night Shift." Tap it to bring up your options.

The two main settings to consider are **Scheduled** vs **Manually Enable Until Tomorrow**.

I prefer the Scheduled option since I don't have to think about it much after I set it up.

The Manual option could be handy if you are going to sleep at an earlier time than usual or you're traveling.

To set up the feature, toggle the switch next to Scheduled. This brings up a time range. Tap to set your own hours – or do what I do – set it to coincide with Sunset and Sunrise. See how automated this can all be? One less thing to worry about while you fall asleep!

Tap **Sunset to Sunrise** under AUTOMATE SCHEDULE, then use the back arrow in the upper left-hand corner to return to the previous screen. Now you're all set up for a restful night!

One more adjustment you might want to make is the intensity of the feature. Try using the slider under COLOR TEMPERATURE to see what you prefer. As you slide it, your screen will change color so you can see what it would look like when Night Shift is enabled.

Again, this is a personal preference. I tend to like mine right in the middle, but you might prefer a cooler or super warm looking screen. It's all up to you!

Now that you have Night Shift set up, you can quickly enable and disable it from Control Center.

Just 3D Touch the brightness slider once again and look for the Night Shift option. Tap to enable Night Shift immediately, or check to see when it is scheduled to go off or come on again.

Enjoy your sleep!

50

Customize what you see in Control Center

Control Center is a powerful and useful tool on the iPhone. You can control settings in a tap that might otherwise take a lot of navigating to find elsewhere.

To make it truly useful for you, let's take a second to set up what you see in Control Center.

First, let's see what's in there.

On an iPhone without a home button, swipe down from the top right of the screen to bring up Control Center.

On an iPhone with a home button, swipe up from the bottom of the screen to bring up Control Center.

You'll see a bunch of toggles, switches, buttons and sliders.

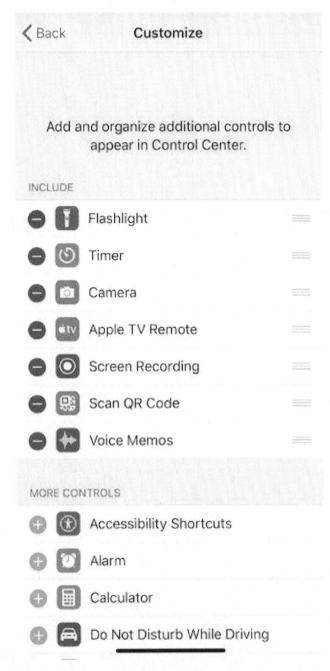

Customize what you see in Control Center

Think of each of these buttons as little shortcuts to perform actions that might otherwise take a few steps.

To customize what you see here, go to **Settings > Control Center** and look for the option to Customize Controls.

In here you'll see all of the things that are currently included in your Control Center, plus the ability to add even more shortcuts.

Some of my favorites to add are the Apple TV Remote, Low Power Mode, Screen Recording and Voice Memos.

Feel free to add whatever works for you by tapping the green plus sign next to a control. This will add it to the list at the top of the screen. If you don't need something in your Control Center, tap the red circle with the line through it to remove it.

Once you're done adding and removing items, you can use the grab tool to the right of an items name to organize the order of each item's appearance.

Tap and push down on the three little lines to the right of the same, then drag to the position you'd like them to be in. Repeat this process until you're happy with your selections and placement, then tap the back carrot in the upper left-hand corner of your screen to save your selections.

Now, swipe to bring up Control Center to see your handy work. The items that you added, removed and re-arranged appear under the main controls and look like a row of app icons. Keep in mind you can't change the location of certain Control Center items, they have to stay where Apple placed them.

Buttons in Control Center usually have dual functionality. You can tap them once to toggle a feature on or off, or you can 3D Touch them for even more functionality.

Now, blast off!

51

Stop those annoying WiFi popups

I can't tell you how many times I've watched people swat away those annoying WiFi network notification pop-ups while they use their iPhone.

Many years ago, this might have been a useful way to join a nearby network, but these days many of us have unlimited data plans or we are simply more discriminating about the open WiFi networks we join.

Just because a network doesn't require a password doesn't mean you should join it. It's a good idea to be critical of any random network in general due to hacking and security concerns.

Also, once you've had your phone for a bit you're probably

not in the habit of joining new WiFi networks all the time unless you are a road warrior.

With this in mind, it's time to turn off this annoying little feature once and for all.

Go to **Settings** > **Wi-Fi** and look for the option that says "Ask to Join Networks." Green means it's on. One tap will turn it off.

The next time you need to join a WiFi network, just go back into **Settings** > **Wi-Fi** and locate the network in the list you want to join. Then, tap its name and enter your password to connect.

While we're on the topic of WiFi, if you join a network that turns out to be a mistake, there's a way you can keep your phone from reconnecting to it.

Press the little "i" located in a circle next to the WiFi network's name. Now, choose the option at the top to "Forget This Network" and your phone won't automatically connect to it again unless you tell it to.

Turn this setting off so you don't see WiFi pop ups

52

Turn off WiFi Assist to save data

The iPhone does a nice job of switching between WiFi and cellular data, but it's not always perfect.

Sometimes you're connected to a WiFi network that just isn't very good. There might be a strong signal, but the actual performance of the network can be poor. This can result in hanging connections, incomplete downloads and web pages that fail to load.

For this reason, Apple built in a safeguard that lets your iPhone fall back on your cellular connection in times like this.

The feature is called **Wi-Fi Assist**, and when Apple first introduced it, people went nuts.

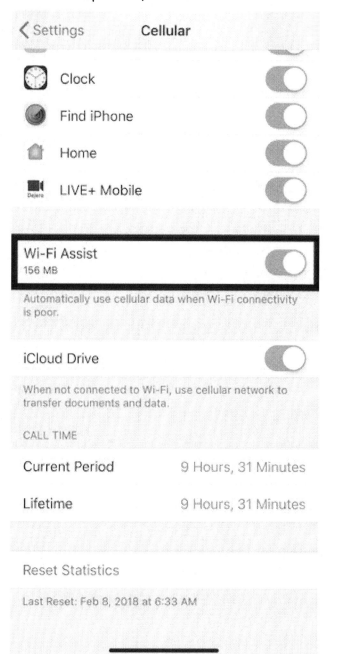

Love it or hate it: Wi-Fi Assist

That's because it was turned on by default, and people noticed their cellular data was still being used even when they thought they were on a WiFi connection.

Thankfully, you can turn this feature off completely, but you have to know where to look to find it.

First, go to **Settings** > **Cellular**. Now, scroll all the way down past the list of apps until you see an option labeled Wi-Fi Assist.

It's the section with the explanation "Automatically use cellular data when Wi-Fi connectivity is poor."

If it's green, that means the feature is toggled on. If you have an unlimited data plan, I'd leave it this way for the best data connectivity experience on your phone.

When it was first launched, many people blamed Wi-Fi assist for using up all of their precious data. You can now check to see how much data it's actually using.

Once the feature has been on for a while, go back into these settings and look right below the Wi-Fi Assist – it will tell you how much "extra" data the feature has used that month. If you don't see anything, it hasn't used any yet.

Keep in mind, Wi-Fi Assist won't activate with certain third-party apps that might end up using a lot of data, like those that stream movies, music or download large email attachments.

Personally, I would leave Wi-Fi Assist on for the best data performance on your iPhone, but turn it off if you are concerned about the feature using up data unnecessarily, especially if you are on a limited data plan.

53

Rearrange CarPlay icons

CarPlay is one of my favorite features of the iPhone.

Sure, you have to have a newer model car to take advantage of it, but more and more people are getting access and realizing just how handy it is.

CarPlay is like having your iPhone on your dashboard screen.

There's really no setup involved in using CarPlay. You just plug your phone into your car with a Lightning Cable and it will either pop right up or you'll have to press something on screen to activate it.

From here, you can see your Phone, Music, Maps, Messages, Now Playing and more.

In just a few taps you can access your most important functions or use Siri to control it all.

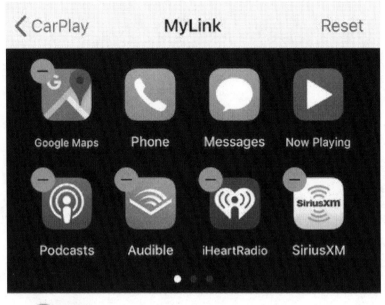

Rearrange CarPlay icons

You can customize this experience – not fully, but just enough to make it yours.

For starters, not every app will show up in CarPlay. The apps that are supported will just show up as you download them to your iPhone. iOS 12 now includes support for third-party navigation apps. See the separate tip on setting them up.

Keep in mind, you can swipe between screens in CarPlay just like you can on the iPhone.

What many people don't realize is that you can also rearrange the order in which the apps appear on their car's display.

To do this, go into **Settings** > **General** > **CarPlay**.

In here, you'll see a list of the cars you've activated CarPlay on. For me, it's my primary vehicle and a rental car I recently had. I'll explain how to remove old cars in a bit.

Tap the name of the car display you want to customize and you'll see your car's screen displayed. From here, you tap and hold on an icon to re-arrange it. Just tap until it "lifts up" and then move it to a new position.

The icons don't wobble as they might on your home screen, so it might take a bit of getting used to. Remember, you can place them on additional screens too.

Don't want an app icon to appear at all? Tap the option to delete it. This is the little circle with the line in the middle of it that's displayed to in the upper left-hand corner of the app's icon. The app will move to a little row under your car's screen. Think of this as a dugout for the apps you don't need right now on the CarPlay screen.

If you ever do, just drag them back onto the black part of the screen while you sing "Put me in, coach!"

If you are totally unhappy with your changes and can't bear to drive ever again with a CarPlay screen that's so disorganized, just tap the Reset button in the upper right-hand corner of your screen. You'll be asked to confirm your move with a message that says Reset Home Screen Layout. Tap it to put everything back in its original place.

Finally, if you're like me and you have a rental car or two displayed in your list of CarPlay cars, just hit the **Forget This Car** option toward the middle or bottom of the customization screen.

And please, don't text and drive.

54

Check your battery health

There is an entirely new section of your iPhone dedicated to teaching you all about your Battery.

Apple originally added it in response to their controversial move to slow down aging phones so they perform more consistently with weaker, older batteries.

That rationale is fine, but people were understandably upset when they found out Apple was, in effect, slowing down their older phones.

Now, Apple gives you much more insight into how your battery is performing, and whether the performance capability is being affected, along with options to bypass the management.

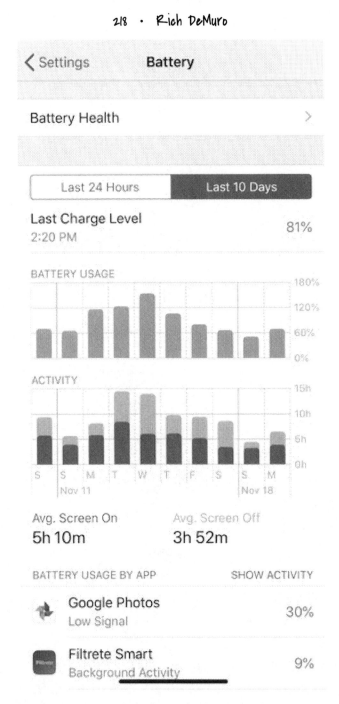

See which apps are using up the most battery

To see the new Battery Health information, go to **Settings** > **Battery**.

Immediately, you'll see a screen filled with information about your battery usage in the **Last 24 Hours**, as well as the **Last 10 Days**.

It's probably more information than you need, but you can see which apps are using the most battery, as well as how long your screen is usually on and off for a typical charge cycle.

This could be useful if you're noticing a lot of battery drain and want to see if a particular app is the culprit.

The other section is labeled **Battery Health**.

Tap in here to see the capacity of your battery and if there is any performance throttling going on.

Maximum Capacity will show you a percentage. This is not the same thing as the battery percentage you're used to seeing that show you how much battery is left on your charge.

This percentage tells you how much battery capacity you have left compared to when the battery was brand new.

For instance, 100% means your battery is doing great.

80% means your battery is holding less of a charge than it used to when it was new.

❮ Battery **Battery Health**

Phone batteries, like all rechargeable batteries, are consumable components that become less effective as they age. Learn more...

Maximum Capacity   100%

This is a measure of battery capacity relative to when it was new. Lower capacity may result in fewer hours of usage between charges.

Peak Performance Capability

Your battery is currently supporting normal peak performance.

Check your iPhone's Battery Health

The part you'll be most interested in is the section labeled **Peak Performance Capability**. It's here where you can tell if Apple is applying any slowdowns to your phone and you have the option to turn off this throttling.

So what is Apple doing, exactly?

According to a support document, a lot. If this feature is turned on, apps might take longer to launch, your screen might be a bit dimmer by default, your volume might be lower and apps might not refresh as often in the background. Things that aren't affected include call quality, GPS location data and the quality of your photos and videos.

Under Peak Performance Capability, you'll see a few different explanations.

You have to read the fine print to know exactly what's going on.

It could say "Performance management applied" along with an option to Disable it. If you see this, that means that Apple's software has determined your battery isn't as good as it used to be and you'll have a better experience if your iPhone manages power consumption a bit by doing the things mentioned above.

You can turn off this performance management, but once you do that, you won't be able to turn it back on. Only your iPhone will be able to turn the performance management back on if it runs into a problem like an unexpected shutdown.

Until then, you'll see the message Performance management turned off.

You might also see a message **Battery health unknown**. If you see this, you probably want to take your phone in for servicing or a replacement battery. I'd recommend doing this if you have an older phone and the software is saying Performance management applied.

Apple is charging $29 for out of warranty battery replacements for many models through December 31, 2018. After that, the price goes up to cost between $49 and $79, depending on your iPhone model.

55

Make the iPhone less animated

A few years ago when Apple first introduced a feature called parallax – where icons and backgrounds seemingly shifted when looked at from various angles – iPhone users actually complained it made them sick.

I can't say that's happened to me, but there are a lot of animations in recent versions of iOS. If they feel a little gratuitous, here is the way to turn them off.

First, let's take a look at some of the motions I'm talking about.

Tap an app to launch it. Notice how it sort of "expands" out of its app icon?

Now, swipe up to get rid of it. See how it sort of diminishes back into its icon?

Lock your phone and then open it. See how the lock screen fades away while the icons slowly contract into place?

Now, move your phone back and forth as you look at the icons on the home screen. Notice how the background might be changing slightly as if the icons are hovering over it?

These are all motions and parallax built into the iPhone and turned on by default.

If you prefer a more basic experience with less movement and transitions, go to **Settings** > **General** > **Accessibility**.

Look for the option labeled "Reduce Motion" and tap it. Now, slide the toggle on to activate the option.

Once you activate this, there is a secondary option that appears called Auto-Play Message Effects. This deals with the way Messages show up and animate.

You have the option to leave these fun features on or turn them off as well. If you turn them off, you'll see a little prompt under animated iMessages that says Replay along with the effect chosen.

Exit the settings screen and you'll instantly notice the changes. Apps sort of just fade in and out when you launch and exit them instead of animating open or away.

On your home screen, you won't see your App icons floating over a moving wallpaper. Everything is just a little more relaxed, with fewer motions and animations to distract you.

It might even feel like your phone is a bit faster.

If you want the animations again, just head back into **Settings** > **General** > **Accessibility** and toggle the switch next to **Reduce Motion** back on again.

It's really just a matter of preference – unless all the movement makes you feel like you're on a ferry to Catalina, New York City or the Puget Sound.

⟨ General   **Accessibility**

VISION

VoiceOver	Off ⟩
Zoom	Off ⟩
Magnifier	On ⟩
Display Accommodations	On ⟩
Speech	⟩
Larger Text	Off ⟩
Bold Text	
Button Shapes	
Reduce Transparency	Off ⟩
Increase Contrast	Off ⟩
Reduce Motion	On ⟩
On/Off Labels	
Face ID & Attention	⟩

Toggle off for less animations

56

Turn automatic downloads on or off

If you have more than one iOS device, you've probably had this happen: You download an app on your iPhone and next thing you know it appears on your iPad.

This is thanks to a feature called **Automatic Downloads**. Apple will automatically download new items you purchase, including free apps, on the other devices you have. For this feature to work, you have to be signed into the same iCloud account on each device. This is why you might notice a game your kid downloads on their iPad shows up on your iPhone.

Apple enables this feature by default, but I find that it's not always useful.

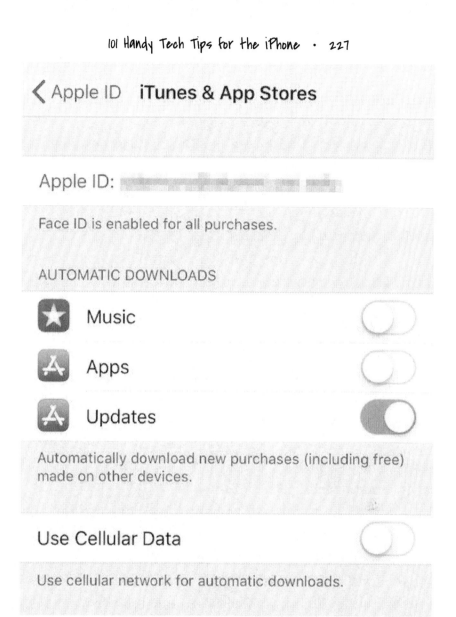

Turn off items you don't want showing up on your other devices

For starters, I think some apps are better suited for different platforms. I might download a paint program on my iPad to take advantage of the larger screen real estate and don't need that app on my iPhone as well.

You can turn this feature off by going to **Settings** > **Apple ID, iCloud, iTunes & App Store** > **iTunes & App Store** > **AUTOMATIC DOWNLOADS**.

By default, Music, Apps and Updates are turned on. You can toggle them off by tapping the little switch to the right of them.

Green means items will automatically download to your various devices, white means the feature is off.

I like to turn off **Apps and Music** but leave **Updates** on. This way, your devices will attempt to automatically download any new App updates in the background to help you keep your Apps up to date.

There is one more component to this and that's **Use Cellular Data**. If it's turned on, your device will use Cellular Data – e.g., data from your wireless provider like Verizon or T-Mobile – to download Apps and Updates.

I like to leave this turned off to conserve my data plan. If you turn it off, your phone will only download automatic updates when it is connected to a WiFi network.

Even with automatic app updates turned off, you can still download an app that you paid for to multiple devices without paying for it again. Just make sure you're signed in with the same Apple ID when you search for the app in the App Store or see the tip about sharing purchases with household members.

57

Free up iPhone storage fast

If you want to reclaim storage on your iPhone fast, there is a handy little built-in tool that can help.

You'll find it by going to **Settings** > **General** > **iPhone Storage**. This will show you a nice little graph showing you how much storage is taken up on your phone, along with the categories taking up space. It could be Apps, Media, Photos, Mail and more.

Under this colorful chart is a list of recommendations to help you free up storage fast. Be sure to hit SHOW ALL to see all of the recommendations for your device.

Now, scroll down a bit and look at the list of apps on your phone.

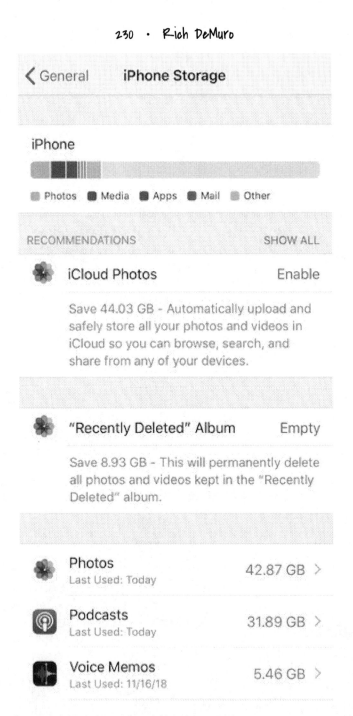

See what's taking up storage on your phone

They are ordered by how much storage they are taking up on your device. Not the app itself, but the files inside the app. This could be items you've downloaded, like videos and music, or photos and other files the app generates over the course of its operation.

For instance, Podcasts is taking up nearly 30 gigabytes on my phone. If I was running out of space and needed to download some new movies for a long flight, I could easily delete some of the files inside this app to free up space.

Likewise, Spotify is taking up nearly 10 gigabytes while YouTube is using nearly 8.

If I tap one of these apps, I get even more details about the space it is occupying on my phone. For instance, with the Podcasts app, the app itself is only 26 megabytes. But the audio files it has downloaded are the 30 gigabytes. I wouldn't worry too much about the option to "Offload App" as it will only save you a bit of space on your phone.

If you no longer need the app at all, you could use the option to "Delete App." This will get rid of the entire app, along with any of the files it was storing and free up all the space it was consuming on your phone. Just keep in mind this might cause a headache if you want the app back again – your files won't come back with it.

Another option, if the app supports it, is to take a look at the list of files the app is storing on your phone. In my Podcasts app, the top three podcasts are consuming 10 gigabytes of files. I can easily delete these to free up some space and download just the episodes I want to listen to again later.

To get rid of one of these files, just swipe left to bring up a button to delete it. If you want to get rid of multiple files quickly, hit the Edit button, then tap the little red icon that pops up to reveal the delete button.

Now, let's take a look at some of the other recommendations at the top of the main iPhone Storage screen. I have recommendations to Enable iCloud Photos, Empty the "Recently Deleted" Album and Review Personal Videos. Each one of these options can save me tens of gigabytes of storage.

The easiest way to free up storage fast is to empty the "Recently Deleted" Album. These are the pictures you deleted from your Camera Roll. iPhone actually keeps them for 30 days before actually deleting them in case you want something back. If you're absolutely sure you no longer need the items you deleted, this could free up some space instantly.

Be a bit more careful with the "Review Personal Videos" option. This will show you the videos in your Camera Roll from biggest to smallest, along with the option to delete them one by one to free up space. Just keep in mind, when you delete an item here it is gone instantly.

58

Delete old backups taking up your iCloud storage

iCloud is probably one of the most misunderstood features in any Apple product, but particularly on iPhone. As they say in the relationship world, it's complicated.

One of the biggest problems people have with iCloud is that they're always running out of space. Part of the issue is that Apple gives users just 5 gigabytes of free cloud storage but typical phones have at least 32 gigabytes of onboard storage. Do the math and it doesn't really work out.

If you are running out of space in iCloud, there is a

somewhat hidden place you can check to see if there might be some old files you can delete: a section containing your old iCloud backups.

You see, every time you set up an iPhone or other Apple device and activate iCloud, your device is generally backed up each time you charge it and the WiFi is on (usually overnight). This is handy when you mess up your phone, lose your device or upgrade and need to copy all of your stuff over to the new device.

Problem is, even after you've copied everything over, Apple doesn't delete your old backup. But you can in and manually clear them out.

First, go into **Settings** on your iPhone and tap the top option that says your name along with Apple ID, iCloud, iTunes & App Store.

Once you're in here, tap the section labeled **iCloud**. You will see a section labeled STORAGE that shows what is taking up all of your iCloud space including things like Backups, Messages, Docs and other items.

If Backups is a large part of the bar graph, you already have a good hint as to what we're going to do next.

Now, tap the section right underneath this graph that says **Manage Storage**. This will take you to yet another screen with the same bar chart, along with all kinds of useful data on what's taking up your iCloud storage.

The section we're most interested in here is the one labeled **Backups**. Tap it to see what's going on. This will take you to yet another screen that lists how much total space your Backups are taking up in iCloud. That's the number at the top.

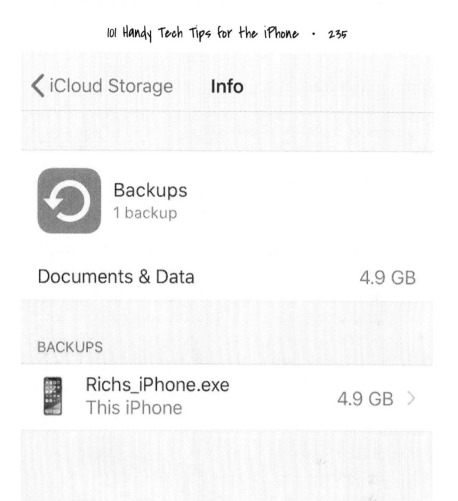

Check for old backups taking up precious iCloud storage

Underneath, you'll see a section labeled BACKUPS that should contain at least one device – the iPhone you're currently using a daily. Under it, you'll see the words "This iPhone."

You don't want to delete this backup, it's the one that contains your most recent data on the phone you use every day.

But below that device, if there are other, older devices listed, they might be fair game to get rid of. These could be old backups from your last iPhone before you upgraded, an old iPad or iPod Touch. You'll see how much storage each backup is taking up in iCloud right next to the name.

If you find a backup you no longer want or need, just tap it for more details including the Last Backup date, size and an option to delete it.

If you're absolutely positively sure that you no longer need a particular old backup, hit the Delete Backup option to reclaim that space in iCloud.

Keep in mind there is no way to get it back once the backup is gone, so be sure you are completely finished with that device's data before confirming.

Let me give you an example of this – let's say you recently upgraded to a new iPhone (Rich's iPhone Xs) and restored it from a backup of your old iPhone (Rich's iPhone 8).

All of your old iPhone data is now on your new iPhone, but the backup of the old iPhone (Rich's iPhone 8) is still taking up space in iCloud.

You can safely delete the old iPhone backup (Rich's iPhone 8) because all of your data is still in two places – your new phone (Rich's iPhone Xs) and in an iCloud backup (Rich's iPhone Xs).

Confusing enough?

One thing to note here – if the size of your current device's backup is close to or larger than your iCloud storage space, you're going to get those message pop-ups that say you need more iCloud storage. There isn't much you can do except pay a little extra each month to get more storage space on iCloud.

Just remember to clear out those old backups once in a while so you're not wasting precious iCloud storage space.

PART VI

Photos

59

Store more photos on your phone

If you find yourself constantly running out of storage on your iPhone, chances are your photos are part of the problem. I've had so many people come to me to ask how they can free up space on their phone, but one look at the numbers reveals an uphill battle.

Apps continue to get larger and 4K videos can chew through storage space fast.

It's possible to get by with the storage you have on board, but it helps to offload some of your photos to iCloud. Thankfully there is a fast and easy way to to do this.

Apple calls the feature **Optimize iPhone Storage**. Turn it on and it can potentially free up a lot of space on your device.

The secret: your iPhone will automatically upload all of your full resolution photos and videos to iCloud, but still keep a smaller copy that you can always see on your phone.

When you tap the picture or go to send it to a friend, the larger version is retrieved from the cloud seamlessly in the background.

To you, it still looks like your photo collection is business as usual.

To turn it on, go into **Settings** > **Your Name** (Apple ID, iCloud, iTunes & App Store) > **iCloud.**

The bar chart at the top tells you how much storage you are using in your iCloud account – remember, this is all stored online. Your iCloud storage could be 200 gigabytes while your phone is only 32 gigabytes.

Now, take a look at the next section labeled APPS USING ICLOUD.

The first one should be **Photos**. Tap here.

The next screen will take us into our Photos setting for iCloud.

If **iCloud Photos** isn't turned on, turn it on. This will upload all of your photos to secure backup online. It's your first line of defense if you lose your phone.

The next setting is the important one. Be sure that **Optimize iPhone Storage** is checked. If it's not, tap it to activate the option.

‹ iCloud   **Photos**

ICLOUD

iCloud Photos

iCloud Photos will be deleted from iCloud in 13 days.
Choose Download and Keep Originals below to download
a complete copy of your photos and videos.

Optimize iPhone Storage   ✓

Download and Keep Originals

If your iPhone is low on space, full-resolution photos and
videos are automatically replaced with smaller, device-
sized versions. Full-resolution versions can be
downloaded from iCloud anytime.

Upload to My Photo Stream

Upload your last 30 days of new photos and view them
on your other devices using My Photo Stream. Photos
from other devices can be viewed in the My Photo
Stream album, but are not automatically saved to your
library.

Shared Albums

Create albums to share with other people, and subscribe
to other people's shared albums.

Be sure Optimize iPhone Storage is on so you don't run out of room
on your phone

This means that your iPhone will automatically manage how it stores photos on your phone and on the cloud.

If you have a bunch of storage on your iPhone and enough for all of your pictures, it won't do anything. But, if you start running out of space on your phone, your iPhone will begin offloading some of your pictures to the cloud.

Again, you can still access them just as usual, but the file won't physically reside on your device, it will be in the cloud.

With Optimize iPhone Storage checked, you can basically have unlimited photo storage on your phone. You're only limited by how much iCloud storage you purchase.

When you go to share or download a photo, your phone quickly grabs the original, full resolution copy from the cloud and it's back on your phone instantly.

If this is the first time you're turning on iCloud Photo Library, it will take a while for all of this magic to happen. Your iPhone will start uploading all of your photos to iCloud in the background, so make sure you have a good WiFi connection.

You can see this progress by opening the Photos app, then tapping the Photos section at the bottom of your screen.

Under the last photo you've taken you'll see data about how many pictures you have on your phone, as well any progress about uploading them to the cloud.

If you're not on WiFi, you can choose to Resume the process if you want to use your cellular connection. If you're on WiFi, you can Pause the process.

Keep in mind, for this plan to fully work, you might need to purchase some extra iCloud storage to back up your entire collection in the cloud. It's worth it.

Once you turn on this feature, you should never run out of storage space on your phone again due to photos.

One note before you send me angry emails explaining that Google Photos can do something similar and it's totally free. You are correct, but this is a book about getting the most out of the iPhone with the software that is already on there.

With just about every tip I'm sharing there is an alternative thanks to an app you can download, but the focus here is on built-in functionality. Still, I don't mind if you download Google Photos and have it backup your photos in addition to iCloud. They should be in at least two places anyway for a proper backup!

60

Swipe up on a photo to do some fun stuff with it

You can do a lot more with the photos you take on your iPhone – and all it takes is a swipe!

You can add cool effects, see the location where they were taken and even the people inside in the pictures. Let's see how to do it.

For starters, take a photo using the **Camera** and then tap to view it, or just go inside the **Photos** app and select a photo you previously took on your iPhone.

Now, swipe up on the photo.

Effects

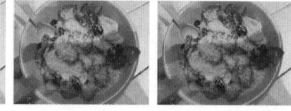

Bounce   Long Exposure

Places   Show Nearby Photos

Swipe up to add Effects to photos

Immediately, you'll see a whole bunch of new options presented for this photo – the first is **Effects**.

If you took a "live" photo, you'll see a preview of several little fun effects you can apply to your picture.

This includes **Loop**, **Bounce**, and **Long Exposure**.

These effects can really change the dynamic of your picture – feel free to play around with them and select one – you can always revert back to your standard photo again later.

Once you select an effect, it is applied to the photo. Now, when you scroll through your camera roll, you'll see the photo with that effect applied.

If you want to go back to your regularly captured photo, just swipe up and tap Live.

Keep in mind, you won't see any of these cool effects for your photos when you swipe up if you have turned **Live Photos** off. Live Photos is an Apple feature that captures a little bit of movement before and after you snap the shutter to take a picture.

To see if that option is turned on or off, go to your Camera and check the little icon with the circles inside of circles. It's right next to the flash icon.

Live Photos is turned on when it's highlighted in Yellow. If you see the circles with a little line through them, the feature is turned off.

I know lots of people don't want to turn Live Photos on since it uses slightly more storage on your iPhone per picture, but I highly recommend leaving it on since it can really help you get more out of your photos.

OK, back to the swipe up options. Experiment with all of them to see how they make your photos more fun. The Long

Exposure is particularly neat for things like waterfalls or night shots that involve cool lighting.

The next section is **Places**. This section reminds us that all photos we take with iPhone carry location information inside them. In here, we can see where the photo was taken on a Map and also see other photos taken near the same location.

After Places is a section called **Related**. These are little albums iPhone automatically creates for you that may or may not be related to the photo your viewing.

Finally, the last option at the very bottom of your screen is **Show Photos from this Day**. Tapping this will bring up all of the photos you took on this particular day. It can be handy to help you find another picture you took that day if you can't find it in another way.

Who knew so many options lurked under your photos? Just remember: swipe up to do more with your pictures, whether it's seeing the location they were taken at or to add fun effects.

61

See all of your selfies

Want to see all of the selfies you've ever taken on your iPhone fast?

No? OK, then skip to the next tip!

For those of you sticking around, here's how to see all of your self-portraits (and many other categories of photos) in seconds!

First, open the **Photos** app.

At the bottom of the app, there is a row with options including **Photos, For You, Albums and Search**.

Tap the option for **Albums** to bring up a section at the top labeled **My Albums**.

If you don't see this at first, tap the Albums option again a few times to back out of whatever Album you are in. Keep tapping until you see My Albums at the top.

+   **Albums**

Media Types

🎥	Videos	80 >
👤	**Selfies**	**120 >**
◎	Live Photos	485 >
⬡	Portrait	44 >
☀	Slo-mo	2 >
📓	Bursts	14 >
📷	Screenshots	90 >
◊	Animated	2 >

Other Albums

⬆	Imports	0 >
👁	Hidden	1 >
🗑	Recently Deleted	148 >

Photos   For You   Albums   Search

See all of your Selfies under Media Types

Now, scroll down the screen a bit. You should see **Shared Albums,** then **People & Places,** and finally, **Media Types.**

iPhone automatically categorizes your photos in lots of different ways.

One of the Media Types should be **Selfies.**

Tap it and you'll see all of the photos you took with your front-facing camera.

Yes, there could be some miscategorized photos in this album. iPhone isn't actually scanning your pics to see if you appear in them, it's just making a guesstimate that if you took it with your front-facing camera, it's probably a selfie.

Before you try to delete a photo that doesn't belong in here, keep in mind it will delete the photo off of your phone completely.

You can use this same tip to see various types of photos including **Videos, Portraits, Slo-Mo Videos, Bursts** and more.

If you take a lot of **Screenshots**, that might be a good album to go through to delete some items you no longer need.

And, on the off chance you don't see a Selfie section under Media Types, consider yourself in the 1% of folks who haven't taken one.

I feel like you deserve an award of some type. Maybe congratulate yourself by taking a celebratory selfie with a big smile on your face?

62

Don't take photos with a filter by mistake

I've seen this happen way too many times – people are taking iPhone photos with a filter applied and they don't even know it!

This could happen because you selected a filter at one time and then forgot to turn it off.

Or, perhaps your kid played with your phone and selected a filter and you started taking pictures without realizing it.

Better yet, maybe your phone was possessed and selected a filter on its own.

OK, that last one probably didn't happen, but you would be surprised how many people come to me with problems on their phones and swear "they didn't do it."

If these circles are in color, you're taking a picture with a filter

I'm not going to judge how it happened, I just want you to be able to fix it.

First, open up the **Camera** app and take a look in the upper right-hand corner or the upper left-hand corner, depending on whether you're holding your phone vertical or horizontal.

Either way, you're looking for the **three overlapping circles** next to the timer icon.

If those circles are black and white, you don't have a filter applied to the photos you're shooting. If it's in color, then you are shooting your pictures with a filter applied.

To remove the filter, just hit the icon with the three overlapping circles, then scroll over to the option for ORIGINAL.

You can now take your pictures.

In the future, before you snap a shot, just take a quick glance at the overlapping circles icon to make sure it's not in color. That is, unless you want to take a photo with a filter.

You have no idea how many events I've been at where I'm watching parents take pictures with a filter unknowingly applied to their shots. Unless they wanted their kid's play captured in DRAMATIC COOL, but I think not.

Now, if you do want to take a photo with a filter applied, just tap the same icon.

This will bring up a bunch of different looks for your photo.

You can scroll through them and you will see a real-time preview of how your image will look with that filter applied.

Even after you take a picture, you can still remove the filter or even apply a new one.

Just go into the **Photos** app, tap a photo that you took with a filter on it, then hit the **Edit** button in the upper right-hand corner.

You should now see options to edit your photo, along with a **Revert** button in the lower right-hand corner.

Tap it to remove the filter you applied when you originally took the photo, confirm your selection and it's gone!

Immediately feeling regret? You can get the same filter back fast!

Just hit **Edit** again and then tap the three little circles under the photo. Yep, the same icon that is on the camera app.

You'll see the same filter options as well as a preview of how the photo will look with one of them applied. Tap to preview the filter, then hit **Done** when you like what you see.

Can't make up your mind? Just go back in and hit **Revert**.

You can really do this all day if you want, think of it as the "circle of life" for photos. Too cheesy? Probably.

63

Press the volume key to snap a photo

Taking photos is probably one of the most popular uses of the iPhone, right up there with iMessages and scrolling through Instagram.

Sometimes, it can be a little challenging to get the perfect shot, especially when you need to position the phone just right AND tap the shutter button without moving very much.

Next time you're shooting in a tricky position, try using the volume button to snap a shot!

Open the **Camera**, then position your grip on the iPhone so you can hold it with one hand while one finger rests on the volume button. It doesn't really matter which one, they will both do the same thing. Now, squeeze the volume button to take a photo.

This trick will allow you to take one-handed photos, which is especially handy for selfies.

By using the volume button to snap a pic, you might find that you shake the camera less when you take a shot, which increases the chance of a sharp photo! When you tap the screen, you move the phone a bit, which could result in a blurry pic.

Alternatively, if you have a pair of headphones on, you can press the volume button on them to act as a remote control to take a picture.

Even better? **Try setting a timer to take a selfie.** This will let you stretch your hand out as far as it can go without worrying about still having to tap the shutter button.

To do it, just go into the **Camera** and tap the icon that looks like a stopwatch.

Tap it to choose from a 3 or 10-second timer.

Now, hit the shutter button and you'll have a nice little delay before your phone automatically takes a picture. There's even a countdown on the screen.

This is a super handy way to take selfies or group shots where you want to fit as many people as possible in the frame, or just get a more creative or steady selfie.

Say cheese!

64

Quickly take a selfie or video

I rarely tap the Camera app to take a photo on my iPhone. Usually, I use one swift motion of taking the camera out of my pocket and then pressing the virtual camera button on the lock screen or swiping left to reveal the camera instantly.

These are just two ways to access the camera fast for a shot you don't want to miss.

Of course, you can always go the old-fashioned route of unlocking your phone, tapping the camera app icon and scrolling through the various photo modes until you find the one you need. There's **Time-Lapse, Slo-Mo, Video** and more. If it's a selfie you're after, you can press the little camera icon with the two circular arrows inside.

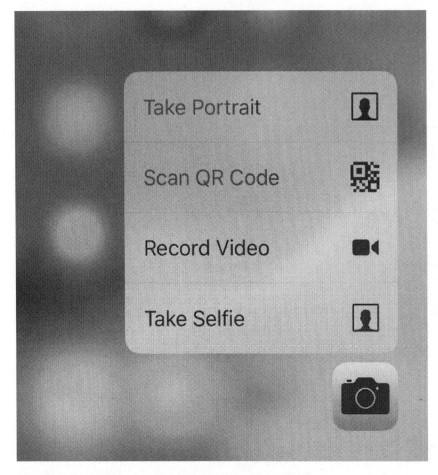

3D Touch the camera icon to jump into a specific mode fast

But there is a faster way to take a Portrait, record video and take a selfie. It's all about the hard press.

For quick access to these modes, you will have to unlock your phone.

But next time, instead of just pressing the Camera icon, press it hard, or 3D Touch the icon.

This will bring up a new menu of expanded options including **Take Portrait, Record Video and Take Selfie.** Record Slo-Mo has been replaced by **Scan QR Code** in iOS 12.

Tap one of these options to enter that capture mode immediately.

65

Adjust the depth effect of a photo

People love the Portrait mode on recent iPhones, and it's pretty easy to see why. You can make a picture look like it was taken by a professional with the subject in focus and the background blurred out. This is the kind of effect that used to take an expensive camera and fancy language to describe: bokeh.

Now, every teenager in America has access to it thanks to the iPhone.

With the latest iPhones and software updates, you can now adjust the blur of the background even after you take the picture.

Adjust the depth effect of a photo after you take it

Try it. Open the **Camera,** then swipe over to **Portrait** mode and take a picture. Keep in mind that even though devices like the iPhone XR can take portrait mode pictures, they are limited to people only since they're using an algorithm to capture the shot instead of two physical lenses, like on the iPhone X and Xs.

Once you're happy with your portrait mode shot, view it full screen and then tap the **Edit** button at the bottom of the picture.

Wait a few seconds and you will see a new slider labeled DEPTH. Drag the slider left or right and watch as the background gets blurrier or more in focus. You can actually adjust the depth effect after you take a picture!

Once you're finished with your changes, you can hit **Done** and the picture will be saved with your new look. Don't worry, you can always go back in and choose a new depth.

If you want to go back to the way the photo was originally captured, you can move the slider back to the tiny dot that denotes the original position. Alternatively, you can hit **Revert** to discard all of your changes.

If you want to see all of your Portrait photos to play with the backgrounds, open your **Photos** app, then hit the section at the bottom labeled Albums. Scroll down to the area labeled **Media Types** and look for **Portrait.** Tap it and you'll see all of the pictures you captured in Portrait mode.

Keep in mind that you might not be able to edit the blurry background effect of all of your Portrait photos, but only the ones that have the extra data written to them, aka, taken with a supported iPhone model.

PART VII

Siri

66

Change Siri's voice

Many of us are familiar with Siri's iconic voice, but did you know you have several options when it comes to how she sounds? You can change her accent and even choose between male or female.

Let's take a listen.

To customize how Siri sounds, head to **Settings > Siri & Search > Siri Voice**.

You'll see ACCENT and GENDER categories.

Under ACCENT, you have choices including **American, Australian, British, Irish** and **South African**.

Tap one of the accents and you'll hear a preview of how Siri sounds with this selection.

Under GENDER, you can tap Male or Female to hear a snippet of how Siri sounds with one of these genders selected.

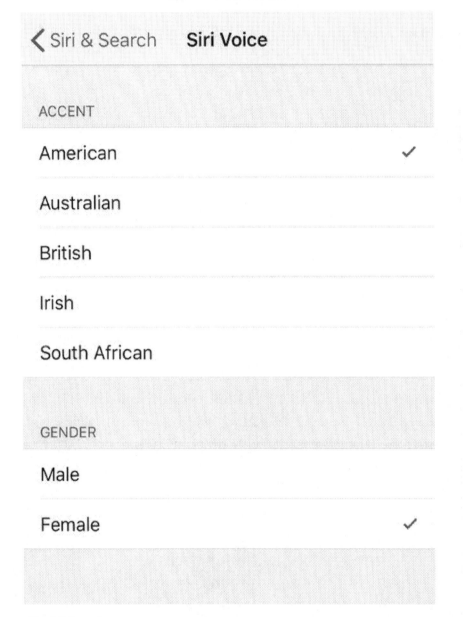

All of Siri's voices

You can take a listen to all of the combinations to find the one that suits you best.

Keep in mind when you tap a new Siri accent or gender, iPhone will download the additional data necessary to serve up the voice.

Whatever you do, don't let your kids find this setting. If they do, you can bet that Siri will sound different every time you pick up your phone.

67

Have siri tell you the news

Siri is good at lots of things, but one of her newer talents is delivering the news. Hopefully, she isn't taking over my job anytime soon, but you can get a quick news update just by asking Siri.

Start by saying something like "Hey Siri, Play me the news."

She'll immediately start playing an audio news briefing from one of several sources.

The first time you trigger this action, she will play the news from a trusted source. You can also switch sources by saying "Hey Siri, switch to Fox News or CNN or The Washington Post. Right now this is about as custom as you can get with this command, but she will remember your preference for news the next time you ask.

This trick also works with other types of news – not just national news. You can say "Hey Siri, let's hear some sports news" and you'll get an update from ESPN.

If you want some music news, just say "Let's Hear some Music News." This one comes from Apple's own Apple Music and Beats 1.

Finally, try asking "Play some Business news." You'll get an update from CNBC.

What is actually happening here is that Siri is pulling up a podcast feed from these providers and instantly downloading and playing it back. It's so fast it's almost magical.

You can pause or otherwise control the audio feed by asking "Hey Siri, Stop" and she will do the job for you. Alternatively, you can go into the Podcasts app and see finer controls in there including back, forward and pause.

This Siri command is a bit different than subscribing to these podcasts in that you can call them up without being a subscriber or even searching for them at all. It's just a fast and easy way to get some news on a broad topic.

This can be especially handy in your car on your way to work. If your phone is connected to your car's Bluetooth or through CarPlay, you can simply start off your commute with some news just by asking Siri.

68

Turn on the flashlight using siri

I'll make this tip quick and easy. You can use Siri to turn the iPhone flashlight on and off. All you have to do is ask.

It might sound silly, but you probably never thought to ask Siri to perform this function. You've locked your phone, gone to the lock screen and hard pressed the little Flashlight icon, or you swiped into Control Center and tapped the icon to turn on the Flashlight.

Next time, just say "Hey Siri, Turn on the Flashlight." Alternatively, you can say, "Hey Siri, turn the flashlight off." Or you can press and hold the side button on your phone to activate Siri and ask the same thing. It's your choice.

Either way, sometimes it's nice to not have to think very much and let Siri do the work.

This could also be handy for finding your iPhone in a dark room, purse, backpack or anytime a little light could help.

69

Ask siri to flip a coin

If you find yourself in a situation where you need to make a decision fast, ask Siri to flip a coin!

It's as easy as saying: "Hey Siri, Flip a coin"

You'll get an immediate answer, whether it's heads or tails.

This can come in handy on so many occasions, and let's be honest, who is carrying around an actual coin these days?

Not sure what shirt to wear, place to go or show to binge?

Let Siri make your decision simple.

She's impartial, instantaneous and never waffles on her decision.

You can even follow up with "Are you sure?"

You'll find out Siri is quite confident in her coin flipping answers, even if some of her other responses are questionable.

Sure beats finding an actual coin

Now, a common sense disclaimer: You probably shouldn't use Siri's Flip a Coin feature for anything that's actually important in life – like the decision to have another child, move to another state for a new job or break up with your significant other.

Siri's answers are purely for entertainment and can't possibly replace consulting with friends, family or anyone you trust.

If you like to play games of chance with Siri, you can also try asking:

"Pick a number from 1 to 100" and she will generate a random number for you.

"Roll a pair of dice" and you'll feel like you're in Vegas minus the cheap drinks and cigarette smoke.

70

---

use siri to help you listen to a podcast instantly

One neat way you can listen to podcasts is to have Siri play them for you.

This is especially handy in the car if you want to use voice control instead of tapping your screen.

It's actually pretty easy, as long as you know the name of the podcast you want to listen to.

Just ask Siri to play it.

For example, you can say "Hey Siri, play the Rich On Tech podcast."

Ask Siri to play a podcast

It will start playing instantly from the Podcasts app.

You can also say "Hey Siri, play my podcasts" or "Hey Siri, play my newest podcasts."

If you want to get really fancy, you can set up a podcast playlist in the Podcasts app and have Siri play that playlist. Except they're not called playlists inside the Podcasts app – they're called "Stations."

To set one up, open the Podcasts app then go to the Library section. Hit the Edit button in the upper right-hand corner and then tap where it says New Station.

Let's name it Morning Commute. Once you do that, you are presented with a whole bunch of customization options. You can specify which episodes to include, just the episodes you haven't played yet, plus you can choose which order your shows will play in. Think of this as your own personal radio station. I have mine set up so I can listen to a little group of tech news podcasts each morning. When you're finished customizing your station, back out of the Settings screen and hit Done.

Now, all you have to do when you get into your car is say "Hey Siri, Play my Morning Commute podcast station." It will play the latest episodes of the podcasts you've specified, in the order you want. When it's finished with the first one, it will go right into the next one. Keep in mind, if want to skip to the next episode in the station list, you can use your steering wheel controls if you're connected to Bluetooth or CarPlay.

It's a pretty amazing feature and once you set it up, you'll really begin to enjoy the convenience of having your own personal radio station, filled with just the news, information and topics you want.

Just to give you some examples of Stations I've set up in the past:

Longer Listens – These are the podcasts that are generally longer in length so when I have more time I'll play this station.

Walking – When I had my first son I would take him for a walk in his stroller each afternoon. It was about a 45-minute walk, so I filled up a station with shows that would roughly add up to this amount of time.

Morning Commute – These are shows that fit into my morning commute. I would start with a quick general news briefing, followed by some key tech news podcasts.

Inspiration – This is filled with fun, inspirational podcasts to get me fired up about working hard and accomplishing my career goals.

The list goes on and on. Get as creative as you want with this!

PART VIII

Tools

71

---

use the built in Level

The Level used to be a somewhat hidden feature on the iPhone, but now it has a new, more prominent home in iOS 12.

You can find it in the new Measure app.

To find it, just open the **Measure** app and look along the bottom of the screen and tap where it says **Level**.

You'll see a big circle with a number in the center of your screen. Tilt your phone to the left or the right and you'll see the numbers change. Play around a bit to see that it works in various directions.

Place your phone on a flat or angled surface to see the angle of degree.

iPhone is the most expensive level ever

My favorite use: Turn your phone sideways and you can now use it to help you straighten a picture frame hanging on your wall!

You can tell when something is level when your screen turns from black and white to green.

This is the part of the book where I will lose you.

That's OK, go ahead and straighten every picture frame hanging around your house.

The next tip will be right here, waiting for you when you're back.

72

—

Store your loyalty cards on a virtual keychain

Do you have a lot of club cards on your keychain?

A feature on the iPhone can help minimize some of those dangling plastic passes, or lessen the load in your real wallet.

While you might be familiar with Apple Pay, there's a related feature that can store various Gift Cards and Store Loyalty Cards right on your iPhone for easy access at checkout.

Keep in mind, not every store or club card is supported, so this could be hit or miss depending on the places you frequent most. Still, lots of common cards are supported like Starbucks, Walgreens, 7-Eleven and Dunkin Donuts. And yes, I just named the four cards I use the most on my iPhone. Your selection may vary.

To start, open the **Wallet** app on iPhone.

Once you're in the app, resist the urge to hit the big blue plus sign in the upper right-hand corner. That is to add credit or debit cards to Apple Pay.

We're interested in the lower section that has to do with Passes. You might have to scroll up a bit if you already have some in here. Look for a smaller button that says **Edit Passes** and tap it.

In this screen, you can clear out any Passes you may have already added, such as any lingering boarding passes or store cards you added at some point but no longer use.

All the way at the bottom of the screen is an option to **Find Apps for Wallet**. Tap here to see the Apps that support Wallet. This can be boarding passes, tickets, reward cards, coupons and gift cards.

Now, just scroll down the list for ideas. You'll see Target, Sephora, Staples, The Home Depot and many of the airlines and movie ticketing apps like Fandango. All of the apps listed support Wallet, and more are being added all the time.

All you have to do is download an app, sign in and look for the logo inside the app that says Add to Apple Wallet. Sometimes it's under the account section or the loyalty card section. You might have to hunt for it depending on how well the app is designed.

Once you've added your card, you can bring up Wallet at checkout fast with – no need to open the individual app up first.

You access your cards at the cash register the same way you would Apple Pay: just a quick double press of the side button on phones without a home button or a quick double press of the home button on phones with a home button.

It might look like this is activating Apple Pay (the same quick double press does open Apple Pay as well) but you can tap the little "stack" of cards towards the bottom of your screen to virtually fan them out. Then tap the card that you want to access to bring it full screen.

Depending on how secure the card is, you might need to enter your passcode, use Face ID or your fingerprint to fully unlock it.

Keep in mind, some cards, like a Starbucks gift card, can be used even when your phone is locked.

This means that someone who finds your phone might be able to get a free latte on your dime.

If you're worried about this, there is a way to turn off the quick access feature, so you can only access your Wallet and cards when your phone is unlocked.

Just go to **Settings** > **Wallet & Apple Pay** and toggle the option to **Double-Click Side Button** or **Double-Click Home Button**, depending on the model of your phone.

This way you can only get to your stored cards after you've fully unlocked your device.

73

Switch to a scientific calculator

The last time I used a scientific calculator was in high school. Thankfully, my career isn't very math dependent, but I did love my TI-84 back in the day.

These days, our phones have absorbed many of the little gadgets we had for specific uses back in the day – the camcorder, tape recorder, camera, tape measure and more are all built into this magical little slab of glass and metal.

But before you download a scientific calculator app to solve that complex equation you're working on, just open up the iPhone calculator. I promise it can handle it!

At first glance, the built-in iPhone Calculator app doesn't seem very advanced, but it is hiding a secret.

Instead of holding your phone up and down like usual, try turning it on its side.

Did the calculator just change? I bet it did!

That's right, in landscape mode, the built-in calculator app becomes a scientific calculator!

I mean, look at all of those buttons that don't mean anything to us non-Beautiful Mind types.

I do recognize sine and cosine, tangent and exponents... all the stuff I promptly forget how to do right after Algebra II.

But if you need this complicated stuff, now you know how to access it!

Overwhelmed? Just turn your phone back to portrait mode and the complicated computation options disappear.

74

Find your lost or stolen iPhone

There might come a time when you misplace your iPhone. Hopefully, this doesn't happen to you, but if it does, you want to be sure you have all the resources available to you to help locate it.

One app that can help is pre-installed on your phone and it's called... drum roll, please... Find my iPhone!

Bear with me, you'd be surprised how many people don't use this, don't set it up or don't know about it.

It's your first line of defense for a lost or stolen iPhone, so make sure you run and set up the app BEFORE you have an issue. You'll thank me later.

To start, open the **Find My iPhone** app on your phone and

log in with your Apple account. You might get a prompt to "Turn on Send Last Location."

It's a good idea to hit the option to **Turn On**. This will allow the app to store the location of your phone for up to 24 hours after the battery has run out.

Additionally, when you set up Find My iPhone, a feature called Activation Lock is automatically turned on. This makes it tougher for someone to activate your device if it's stolen. Even if they erase all of your data, iOS will still require some of your information before they will release the lock and allow the phone to be set up as new.

This is why I don't understand why people still steal iPhones. They're basically useless once they're out of the hands of the owner.

Just make sure you have a strong passcode on your phone or it defeats the purpose of all of this. If it's 1-1-1-1 or 0-0-0-0, a crook with your phone will figure that out in seconds and make your phone theirs.

Now, you might be thinking, wait a second... if my phone is no longer in my possession, how can I use Find My iPhone to find it since the app is on my phone, which is lost?

Good question. That's why you need to buy a second iPhone just to install the app and run it to locate your old phone. Just kidding.

You can access Find My iPhone from the web by going to icloud.com/find.

Here, you can log in with your Apple ID and password. Hopefully, you'll see your iPhone on a map. Of course, you can always use another iOS device to accomplish this like an iPad or iPod Touch.

From here, you can do things like **Play a sound**, which will cause your device to sound an audible alert. I had to do this the other night when my phone went "missing" after dinner. Turned out my wife moved it off of the kitchen table and onto a chair to clean the table. A beeping sound on the phone led us to the misplaced phone. Crisis averted.

If you still can't find it or you believe your phone was taken, you can turn on Lost Mode, which locks your device and puts a message on the lock screen with return instructions. Erase your device will do just what it sounds like.

Keep in mind, your device must be connected to some sort of wireless network for any of these options to work. If it's under a seat cushion in your home, you'll probably hear it beep and you can retrieve it. Or you can see it's last location on a map and realize you left your phone at a friends house.

Usually, you're asked to turn on Find My iPhone during the initial setup of your device, but if you want to make sure that it's activated, head into **Settings** > [Your Name] **Apple ID, iCloud, iTunes & App Store** > **iCloud** and scroll down until you see "Find My iPhone."

Tap it and confirm that the toggles are on for both Find My iPhone and Send Last Location.

Now, just hope you never need to use any of this.

PART IX

Media

75

See all the images you've exchanged with someone

If you use the Messages app a lot, there will come a time when you think to yourself: Didn't so and so send me a picture of that? Now, where is it?

Then you'll proceed to scroll through every message you've exchanged with that person in an attempt to find it. And guess what?

Invariably, you won't.

Here's a much easier way.

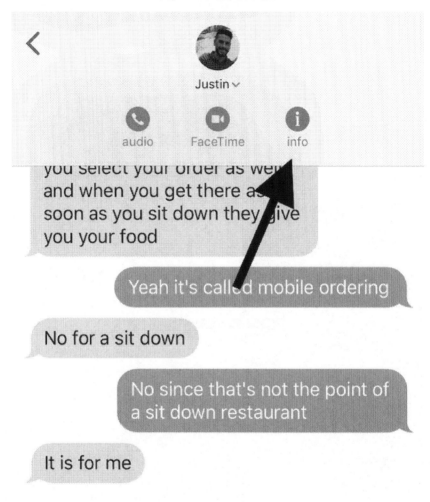

Tap info to see pictures and files you've exchanged with someone

Just go into **Messages,** then tap the conversation of the person you want to see the picture (or file) from.

Once you're in the conversation screen, tap the person's name at the top of the screen. It should have a little symbol like this (>) next to it.

This will reveal some new options, including some other

ways to contact the person. The option we're interested in is labeled **info**. Tap it.

Now, you will get a whole bunch of options but at the bottom of the screen, you'll see a nice little album of all of the **Images and Attachments** you've exchanged with that person over time.

Tap an image to bring it full screen, which reveals some more things you can do with it. There's a share arrow in case you want to save it to your Camera Roll or share through AirDrop or with an app.

Surprised that all of these images and files are here?

You can delete them, too.

When you're on the gallery view, that is, when you're looking at all of the pictures on the screen at once, lightly tap and hold your finger on one.

This will bring up a menu that will allow you to **Copy** or **Delete** individual pictures out of the message history.

If you want to delete multiple pictures or files at once, tap and hold once again, but choose the **More** option. This will allow you to select multiple items. You can then tap the Trash can that appears in the lower right-hand corner to remove the items permanently.

By the way, this tip came in handy for me the other day. Someone had sent me a bunch of pictures that I wanted to save to my camera roll. Instead of doing this process one by one, I went into the section to see all of the pictures we've exchanged, selected all of the pics at the same time and simply used the command to save them. It was super useful and cut out a lot of unnecessary steps.

76

Download an app you bought to another device

Did you know that you can share the Apps you buy on your iPhone with up to six family members? Everyone will need their own Apple ID and according to Apple's rules, be in your household. But once they're linked to your Family Sharing account, if you buy a game for one kid, you can easily download it for another child without paying a second time.

Easy, as in, once you know how to do this and where to look for the feature.

For starters, make sure you've set up Family Sharing and both the account you're buying the app from and the account you want to download the app to are in the same Family Sharing plan.

Confirm this by going to **Settings** > **Apple ID** > **Family Sharing** and you should see both parties listed under FAMILY MEMBERS.

Keep in mind you can create a "Child Account" by tapping the option to Add Family Member...

Before we proceed, a quick note. You have no idea how many families out there don't have Family Sharing set up. I didn't for the longest time. My wife and I should share the same iTunes login on our phones and it would create all kinds of headaches for downloads, iMessage and iCloud. Do yourself a favor and take the time to set up Family Sharing and create accounts for every separate member of your household and link them up. It will make life much easier going forward and way less confusing.

First, pay for and download an app as you normally would on the first device. This could be from your Organizer account, as Apple refers to the person in charge or one of your family member accounts. It doesn't really matter. I prefer to buy the app using my account and then download it to the kids' devices so all apps are in one place under my login.

Once you've purchased and/or downloaded the app to your primary device, pick up the second device you want to download it to.

Open up the **App Store** on the secondary device and tap the section at the bottom labeled Today to go to the App Store home screen.

This should reveal a little circle in the upper right-hand corner of your screen with a profile picture in it. Tap it to go to an **Account** screen.

On this screen, you will see a section labeled **Purchased**.

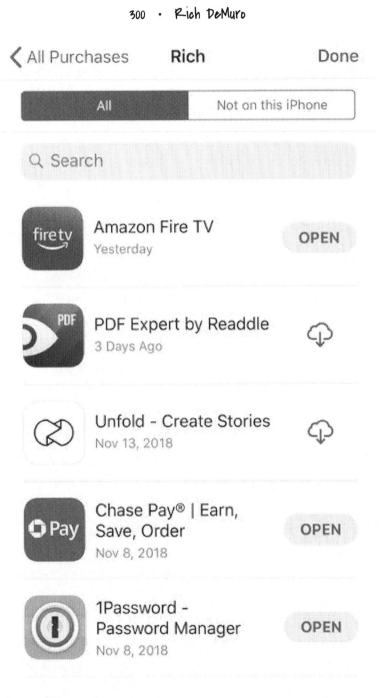

Don't double pay for app purchases

Tap the **Purchased** section to bring up all of the purchases linked to the various accounts in the family.

Tap the family member's name that originally downloaded the app and this will bring up a list of all of the apps they've downloaded, both fee and purchased.

Find the app you want by searching, browsing or using the filter for **Not on this iPhone/iPad** and just tap the icon with the cloud and down arrow.

The app will immediately download to this secondary device, no second payment necessary!

I'm convinced parents around the nation are double and triple spending on their App Store purchases just because this feature isn't very visible or straightforward.

But now you know you never have to buy the same app twice for your family.

77

Download a video you bought to another device

If you read the tip on Family Purchases, you already know that you never need to pay for the same app twice for multiple family members' devices in your household.

The same holds true for Movies and TV shows you purchase from the iTunes Store.

It might not be readily apparent, but if you purchase a movie on your iPhone for the kids to watch, you can easily download it to another household device, even if it's on a separate Apple Account.

First, you must make sure they are linked to your account through Family Sharing.

Confirm this by going to **Settings** > **Apple ID** >

Family Sharing and you should see both parties listed under FAMILY MEMBERS.

You can create a "Child Account" by tapping the option to Add Family Member...

Once you've purchased the media, you're ready to download it to another device. Keep in mind, you can purchase the Movie or TV Show on any account that's linked to Family Sharing. It doesn't have to be purchased on the organizer's account, although I feel like this is the easiest way to keep things in order. Think of this system as having one "master library" and then downloading the same content to your other accounts. But do whatever works for you.

After you've purchased a movie or TV show on the primary device, head over to the secondary device you also want to download it too.

Now, open up the **iTunes Store**.

Along the bottom row you'll see sections including **Music, Movies, TV Shows, Search** and **More**. Tap **More**.

This will bring you to a page with some sections. Look for the one labeled **Purchased**.

Once you tap here, you'll be able to see all of the media you've purchased on any device linked to your family account. Browse in here to find the item you want to re-download. Keep in mind, it could be listed under your account or one of the accounts under FAMILY PURCHASES. It depends where you originally purchased the media.

Items are organized by account name, followed by type: Music, Movies, TV Shows. Browse the appropriate section until you see what you want to download.

Once you tap an item's name, you'll be taken to an iTunes

Store page. Watch closely, as the payment buttons disappear before your eyes and they turn into a **Cloud icon** with a little arrow pointing down. Tap this icon and your Movie or TV show will download to this secondary device for free.

Now you can feel good knowing that you didn't overpay for a TV Show or Movie! There is no need to buy things more than once if you're all in the same household.

78

Quickly see which videos are downloaded

You have no idea how many times I've boarded a plane with nothing to watch on my iPhone. And it's not fun. Because we're mostly on WiFi, our iPhones have a tendency to show us all of the media in our iCloud library that's available to us.

Then, when we get on a plane, we realize everything has disappeared because our phone was actually displaying items from the cloud to play on demand.

Many times, movies and TV shows aren't actually stored on our devices.

Here's the fastest way I know how to check to see if an item actually resides on your device and not in the cloud.

All you have to do is **flip your phone into Airplane mode to check**.

The reason? Your phone can no longer rely on its internet connection to show you everything purchased in your cloud library. You're forcing it to show its cards.

To see how this works, open up the **TV app** on your phone. This is where all of your purchased and rented iTunes media lives. Once you're in the app, tap the section titled Library at the bottom of your screen.

You'll see several items here including **Recently Purchased Shows,** **Recently Purchased Movies** and sections for **TV Shows** and **Movies**.

If you've ever purchased any media through iTunes, it lives here and it's all instantly playable from the cloud. Go into the Movies or TV section where you have a show or movie you've bought.

Tap an item and then press the **Play** button. It should start playing.

Now, flip your phone into **Airplane Mode** and watch what happens. Suddenly, your phone will only display items that are actually downloaded and stored on your device. AKA, stuff you can watch without an internet connection, like on a plane.

Flip your phone into Airplane Mode to see downloaded videos fast

This is the fastest and easiest way you can tell if there is something to watch on your device when you don't have a connection.

Flip Airplane Mode off and watch your library re-populate.

Now, if you want a movie or TV show to be available to you when your connection-less, find the item you want to download and tap it to go to the detail page.

See that little cloud with the arrow pointing down? Tap it to download the item to your phone's storage.

Word to the wise: you will not be able to do this when you are actually on a plane, waiting to take off. The downloads are just too big, and the connections just too slow. Believe me, I've tried many times.

So do it the night before a big trip and make sure the items actually download.

You know how to check, right? Just flip your phone into Airplane mode. If an item you downloaded isn't there, something went wrong.

Keep in mind, this little trick can help you clean up the downloads on your phone!

Now that you know how to see all of the movies and TV shows that are taking up space on your phone, just hard press a TV episode or movie to bring up a box that says "Remove Download." This will delete the item off of your phone and free up space.

As long as it's stored in your iCloud library, you'll always be able to re-download it later.

79

See if a movie or TV show is streaming for free

No one wants to pay to watch a movie or TV show that's streaming free inside one of the services you subscribe to. iPhone has a quick and easy way to find out if something is playing across a variety of apps including HBO GO, Amazon Prime Video, STARZ, Showtime and lots of cable TV channel apps.

After all, if you're already paying to subscribe to a service, why pay to rent something you can see for free?

To start, go into the **TV app** on your iPhone. Tap the **Search** icon at the bottom of the screen.

Now, search for a movie or TV show.

For this example, I'll use the movie *Paul Blart: Mall Cop 2*. If you search for this movie and tap it, you'll see a bunch of information. What we're interested in is what it says right under the genre and year.

If you see several streaming services listed, you might be in luck. These are the places you can stream the title for free or with a subscription to one of these services.

At the time of this writing, I can watch *Paul Blart: Mall Cop 2* on FXNOW, iTunes, FOX NOW and PlayStation Vue.

Obviously, iTunes is paid, but I would be able to stream this movie for free with the other services if I'm a subscriber.

Try searching for another movie or TV show to see where it is streaming as well.

This is a super handy feature and Apple has done a nice job of integrating lots of streaming services.

Once you find something you want to watch, you can just tap the play button to open it in the default streaming app. If you want to open in a different streaming app, just tap the three little dots to the right of the play button.

This will bring up an option to "Open In." Tap it to see all of your streaming app options. Tap one to start playing the item. If you don't have the appropriate app installed on your phone you'll be prompted to install it.

If an item isn't yet streaming on a provider you subscribe to, you can always use this same three dots menu to **Add to Up Next**. You'll be able to easily come back to a movie or TV show later and see if it's now playing on a service you pay for. You can find your **Up Next** list under the **Watch Now** section at the bottom of the TV app screen.

Two more things to know!

First, you have to use the TV app to search for movies and TV shows or you won't see this information. If you search inside the iTunes Store, you will not see the option to stream the movie or TV show on different providers.

Second, not every streaming service is included, so this information isn't foolproof. An item might very well appear on a streaming service but Apple hasn't included it yet. Many popular services are represented, but you can see the current list of providers indexed using the link below.

https://support.apple.com/en-us/HT205321

80

Send Bluetooth audio to a new device

Usually, your iPhone is pretty good at figuring out which Bluetooth device you want to send audio to. It could be a portable speaker or a set of wireless headphones.

The trouble starts there are multiple devices around and your phone just picks the last one you connected to but you want it to connect to another device nearby.

Here's an easy way to direct your audio to the device you want to listen on.

The solution is in the **Control Center**.

Open it up and look for the little box labeled **Music**. It might also contain the name of a song that is playing or recently played.

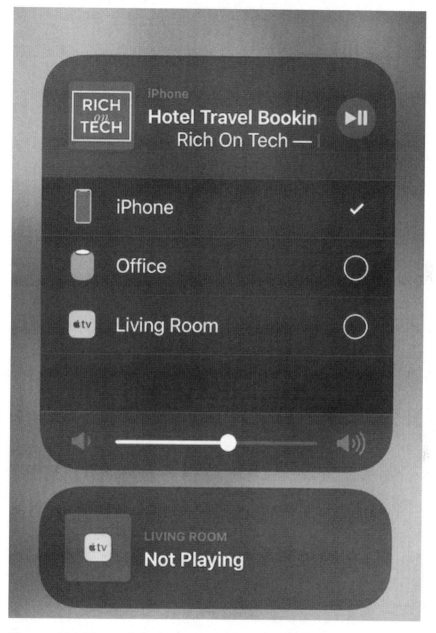

Choose which Bluetooth device you want to send audio to

3D Touch this little box to bring up a bigger version of this little box.

Now, tap the icon in the upper right-hand corner that looks like several circles with a triangle pointing to the center.

Press this little icon to display a list of all of the nearby Bluetooth devices you can play your audio on. It could be a speaker, AirPods, headphones or something else.

If you don't see the device you want to play your audio on, make sure it's turned on and properly paired with our phone. You can do that in **Settings** > **Bluetooth**.

If you have any AirPlay devices on your network, these will be displayed under this box.

Now, just tap any of the available devices and your audio should start playing there. You might have to press the **Play/Pause** button to go back to the previous screen and press Play to get the audio stream started.

From here on out, YOU are in control of your iPhone's audio stream. Send it to a speaker, headphones, or a myriad of other devices. It's your choice.

81

Listen to a podcast

I've been listening to or producing podcasts in some form since just before the original iPhone launched. Back then, you would download audio files and sync them to your iPod. Hence the name, "podcast."

What's a podcast, you ask? Think of it as a radio show but instead of tuning in at a particular time to listen, it starts when you hit the play button on your phone. Podcasts are pre-recorded, so you can play them whenever you have the time. Like on your work commute. Or at the gym. Or on the plane. Or your work commute on a plane if you're super fancy. Or in the gym in a plane on your work commute, if gyms exist on planes. Now I sound like Dr. Seuss.

Anyway, it still surprises me to this day that people have not tried listening to a podcast. Think of a subject. Yep, there's a podcast about it. Whatever you are into, chances are someone has talked about it into a microphone and put it out there for download. It won't even cost you anything to subscribe and listen. I even do one – we'll use mine as an example of how to subscribe.

First, find the app on your iPhone called – wait for it – **Podcasts**. If you've never listened to a podcast, you've probably never even noticed it.

Many times, someone will tell you the name of a good podcast that you "must listen to" and you can just search for it in the Podcasts app and subscribe. Each new episode will be delivered to your phone so you can listen at your leisure.

Let's search for a podcast. Tap the **Search** icon in the lower right-hand corner of the app screen. Then tap in the search box and type in "Rich On Tech." Immediately, Apple will start autocompleting the words for the show title. You can tap on the result or hit the Search button in the lower right-hand corner of your keyboard to complete your search.

The result? You see a list of all the matching shows with similar names. My podcast should be right at the top of the list. Tap on the cover art (it sort of looks like a CD cover from back in the day) and you should see a subscribe button. If you hit Subscribe, your phone will automatically download the latest episode or two so you can listen at any time, even if you don't have a strong WiFi or cellular signal (like on the plane).

〈 Search

Rich On Tech

Rich DeMuro

Subscribed

5.0 ★ ★ ★ ★ ★   2017 – 2018

57 Ratings   Technology

TV Tech Guy Rich DeMuro offers tech tips and
tricks.   more

Recent Episodes

···· SUNDAY

Hotel Travel Booking Secrets

Learn the way to get the best price possible on
your next hotel booking with a little known ag...

Details ━━━━━━━━━ 9 min left

THURSDAY

Amazon's Black Friday Deals; iPhone vs Pixel Camera; Uber Rewards

Amazon announces seven days of early Black...

Hotel Travel Booking...   ▶   ↻

Listen Now   Library   Browse   Search

Listen to a Podcast

318 · Rich DeMuro

If you want to sample a podcast before you commit to a subscription, just scroll down to the Recent Episodes section and tap on one of the episode titles. It will start playing immediately. You can stop it by using the controls that appear near the bottom of your screen.

Once you've subscribed to a show or two, hit the **Library** button at the bottom of your screen to see all of the podcasts that you are currently subscribed to. From here you can play **Recently Updated** episodes or hit **Episodes** to see a list of all of the shows you can listen to. You can further sort them by **Title** or **Date Added**.

To find some more shows, you can use the Browse button at the bottom of your screen. From here you can see **Featured podcasts,** **Top Charts,** **All Categories** and **Featured Providers**. The neat thing about podcasts is that you're not limited to the biggest professional producers. Anyone can produce a podcast and you can get it on your phone. Browse the top charts and you'll see podcasts from big companies and independent creators.

Once you've filled your library, there are lots of ways to listen to your shows. You can head straight into the Listen Now section to see all of your recently updated shows and pick one to play. Or you can head into your Library to see a list of shows in the order they were released, from newest to oldest. It's all up to you!

Just remember that when you're playing a podcast, you can access the full set of controls by tapping in the section right above the buttons at the bottom of your screen. This will bring up a full-screen player with controls to scrub through an episode, skip back or forward several seconds, play and pause your show, as well as adjust the volume. If you're a real power listener, you might want to try the little control with the 1X on it. Tap here to adjust the audio speed of the podcast.

If you're concerned that all these great podcasts will take up a lot of space on your phone, you can adjust the storage settings to your liking. Head into **Settings** > **Podcasts** and you'll see lots of options. My recommendation is to make sure the toggles are on for **Sync Podcasts** and **Only Download on Wi-Fi**. This way new episodes are downloaded over WiFi and don't use your cellular data.

Otherwise, it's really up to you to when it comes to the EPISODE DOWNLOADS section. You can set the Refresh interval and how many episodes are downloaded. Personally, I turn on the toggle to **Delete Played Episodes**, which will purge episodes you've listened to from your phone 24 hours after you finish listening to them. Don't worry, you can always re-download an episode again later.

Now that you know how to listen to podcasts, try listening to mine each day! Imagine cool tech news and tips on a daily basis. Better yet, don't imagine, just listen!

PART X

Productivity

82

Customize what siri Suggestions shows

One of the most useful features on the iPhone is the ability to search through just about every app, contact and other pieces of information stored on the phone with a quick pull down of the screen.

When you do this, you'll notice that you get all kinds of results from various places – The APP STORE, CONTACTS, WEBSITES and items from inside the various apps you've installed.

This search results page can be super useful if it serves up the information you need, but it can also get very cluttered with nonsense apps taking up precious search results real estate.

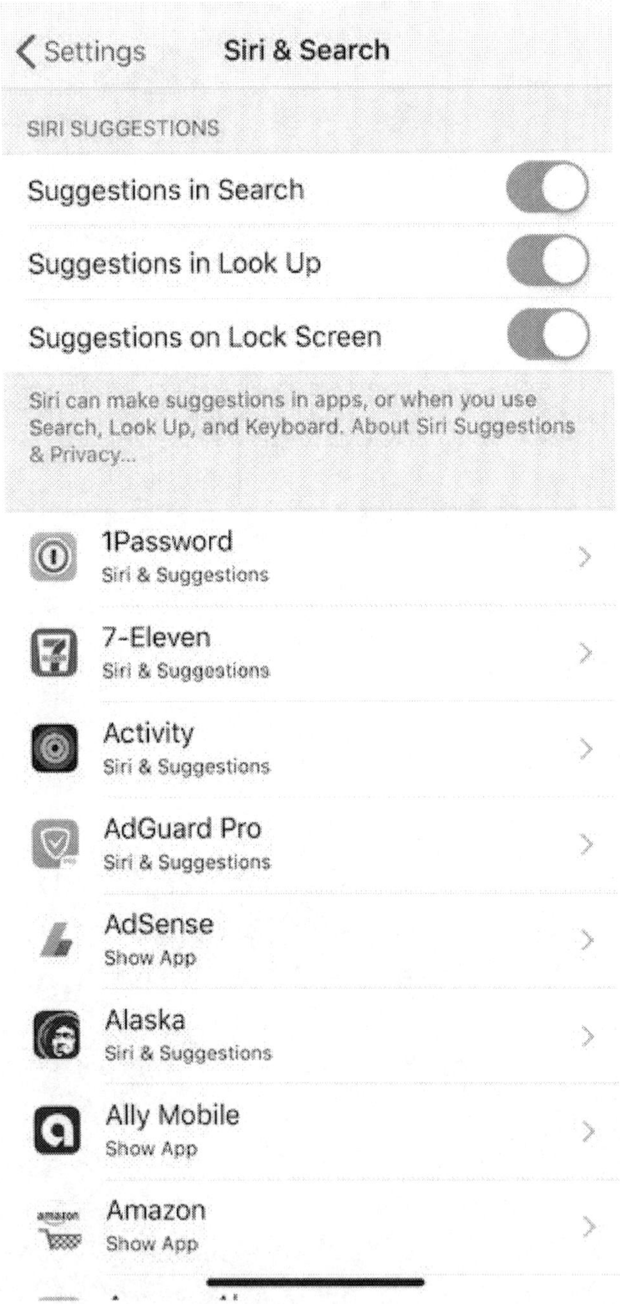
Settings
Siri & Search
SIRI SUGGESTIONS
Suggestions in Search
Suggestions in Look Up
Suggestions on Lock Screen
Siri can make suggestions in apps, or when you use Search, Look Up, and Keyboard. About Siri Suggestions & Privacy...
1Password
Siri & Suggestions
7-Eleven
Siri & Suggestions
Activity
Siri & Suggestions
AdGuard Pro
Siri & Suggestions
AdSense
Show App
Alaska
Siri & Suggestions
Ally Mobile
Show App
Amazon
Show App

Clean up Siri Suggestions

Here's a way to tailor these searches to the information you need the most.

To start, go into **Settings > Siri & Search**.

Scroll down until you see the section labeled SIRI SUGGESTIONS. There are several options here including Suggestions in Search, Suggestions in Look Up and, new in iOS 12, Suggestions on Lock Screen.

I would be sure that all of these are on since Siri actually does a really nice job of anticipating your next move and suggesting the appropriate information or shortcut you need.

Now, take a look at the laundry list of apps under SIRI SUGGESTIONS. This is the list that you will want to clean up.

You see, every app in this list has the potential to appear in Siri's Suggestions, but there might be some apps that you just don't need to do this.

For instance, nothing against 7-Eleven (great coffee!) but I don't necessarily need them in my Siri Suggestions.

On the Flip side, if I'm typing the name of a movie into my search bar, I would like results from Fandango.

And on the other hand, I can probably turn off Jamba Juice results in my searches.

Go through this list of Apps and turn off the appropriate toggles for each app you don't think you need appearing on your lock screen or search results.

Back to my 7-Eleven example, if I turn off the option to "Allow on Lock Screen," I might not see a notification deal on my lock screen when I get near one of their convenience stores. You need to turn these toggles off wisely.

The main thing you're trying to do here is clean up your search results so you can find the stuff you're looking for faster.

If you have multiple movie apps installed, like IMDB and Fandango, maybe you only want results from one when you start typing in the name of a movie.

It's all up to you.

You might notice some apps have an option to **Show App**. If you turn this off, the app won't show up when you search for Apps by name when you pull down on your home screen. I use this action all the time to bring up apps fast as opposed to looking for them on my home screen and inside folders. So I recommend you only turn this off for apps that you don't think you'll ever search for by name.

You can see how this could be useful for hiding apps from a search that you might never look for. There's only room for a few apps in that row of results so the more useless apps you eliminate, the more useful your search results will be with less typing.

Once you're finished going through all of your apps, your search screen should be much easier to handle – highlighting the apps and results that YOU find most useful.

How can you use the pull down to search functionality on your iPhone? Let me count the ways.

Need a contact? Just pull down and start typing their name.

Need fast access to an app? Just pull down and start typing in the name of the app.

This list goes on and on – you can search for a keyword inside one of your notes, a file, movies, emails and much, much more. In my opinion, this is the handiest feature on the iPhone.

Keep in mind, Siri uses artificial intelligence to arrange the results in an order based on how likely the result is to be your top choice – often it's spot on.

83

Share your Internet connection with a WiFi hotspot

In many cases, you can share the internet connection on your iPhone with another, nearby device like an iPad or laptop computer.

The feature is called **Personal Hotspot** and it's simple to set up.

You can use it to let your kid watch Netflix on their iPad or use your laptop anywhere you have a cellular connection on your phone.

Once the feature enabled, your iPhone becomes its own little

WiFi hotspot. It sends out a WiFi network signal that other devices can latch on to, provided you link them up by providing a password you set.

Before you set up your personal hotspot, you might want to check with your wireless carrier to see if it's included in your plan.

Some things to know: even if you're on an unlimited plan, carriers sometimes limit the speeds you can get on the devices you connect through your phone.

This means that even though your iPhone has a speedy connection, your hotspot connection might only be fast enough to send and receive emails or surf the web.

Also, your wireless provider might only give you a certain amount of hotspot data to use each month. Once you use it all up, the hotspot feature might slow down or turn off altogether.

Just call your wireless carrier and ask a few questions:

Do I have a hotspot included in my plan?

What's the speed on the hotspot data?

Is there a limit to the data I can use through my hotspot?

Now, it's time to set your hotspot up. Go to **Settings > Personal Hotspot.**

The first thing you want to do is set a password. You'll notice that your iPhone has already generated a suggested password. Just tap it to change to something that works better for you. Don't make it too easy for others to guess – otherwise, you'll have a bunch of random people using your iPhone to surf the web.

Once you pick a good password, hit **Done** on this screen.

❮ Settings **Personal Hotspot**

Personal Hotspot

Now Discoverable.

Other users can look for your shared network using Wi-Fi and Bluetooth under the name "Richs_iPhone.exe".

Wi-Fi Password vfhmmhevuez3 ❯

TO CONNECT USING WI-FI

1 Choose "Richs_iPhone.exe" from the Wi-Fi settings on your computer or other device.

2 Enter the password when prompted.

TO CONNECT USING BLUETOOTH

1 Pair iPhone with your computer.

2 On iPhone, tap Pair or enter the code displayed on your computer.

3 Connect to iPhone from computer.

TO CONNECT USING USB

1 Plug iPhone into your computer.

2 Choose iPhone from the list of network services in your settings.

Use Personal Hotspot to share your Internet connection with another device

Now, when you want to share your internet with a nearby device, just toggle the switch next to **Personal Hotspot**.

Alternatively, you can also open **Control Center** and 3D Touch the group of icons that contain **Airplane Mode, Cellular, WiFi** and **Bluetooth** connections.

This will bring up even more toggles including the one for **Personal Hotspot**. Just tap to turn it on!

Several things to keep in mind here. First, the hotspot will use more battery on your phone. If you're going to be using the hotspot function for a long period of time I would plug in your phone or have a portable backup battery around.

Also, I would turn off the hotspot feature when you're not actively using it – for battery and security reasons.

So, how do you find your phone from another device?

Go back to the **Settings** > **Personal Hotspot** screen.

You'll notice right under your password it explains how to connect using WiFI. In step 1, it will say the name of your iPhone's WiFi network in quotes.

If this is something super generic like "iPhone" you will probably want to change it.

Just go to **Settings** > **General** > **About** > **Name** and tap the name of your phone to change it to whatever you want.

When you're ready to connect, just flip on the hotspot using the Settings or the Control Center on your phone, then look for your WiFi network on your secondary device. Type in your password and surf away!

If your other device happens to be an iOS device like an iPad, and you're signed into the same iCloud account, you might notice a special PERSONAL HOTSPOTS section in your WiFi settings when you go to connect. In this case, you won't need to enter a password to link the devices, Apple shares it automatically since it knows both devices are yours. Just tap the name of the other device and you're good to go.

84

Search for a keyword in your messages

Apple prides itself on simplicity, but sometimes this can make simple features tough to find.

Case in point: searching for a keyword in Messages.

Lots of people don't even realize you can search through your Messages, while others stumble upon the feature by accident.

If you haven't discovered this basic function on your iPhone just yet, prepare to be pleasantly surprised.

First, open your **Messages** app and look for a search bar. It's not readily apparent.

But, PULL DOWN on your list of messages and suddenly, it's there!

Edit

Messages

Q Search

Pull down on the Messages screen to reveal a search bar

Now, try typing in a search term. It can be someone's name or a keyword you remember in a conversation.

As you type, you'll notice your list of messages quickly pare down to include just the search term. Tap a result and you'll be taken to the location in the message chain where your search term appears in the conversation.

Watch closely – the actual message text where the search word is found will appear in a darker color for a bit, then revert back to normal. This is a subtle cue for you to easily find what you're ultimately searching for on screen.

You can press the X in the circle to start a new search or hit cancel to exit out of search altogether.

Word to the wise – this isn't Google. This simple search functionality works best with a single keyword. Maybe two. Let's say you're looking for "basketball lessons" and you type that in. It will only find multiple words if they are right next to each other. It's best to stick to a single keyword if you're not sure what you're looking for. If you put too many words together you might not have any results at all.

85

Have siri help identify who's calling and texting

This is one of my favorite features of the iPhone and you might even have it turned on without knowing what it's all about.

A few years ago, Apple introduced a way for Siri to search your email and collect information about the people who you communicate with. This way, she can identify them when they call or text you, or offer to add the information to your contacts. It's the reason you see "Maybe:" along with a name next to text message or phone calls. It might sound creepy, but I find it to be one of the most helpful features on the iPhone, especially in our age of Robocalls.

When Apple introduced the feature, they called it something

like Proactive Siri, now they mainly refer to the feature as Siri Suggestions. Either way, it can be a big help.

The magic happens when Siri has access to your email messages. This way, it can look at senders names and email addresses, as well as information in their signature line including email addresses, physical addresses, phone numbers and more.

For this to work, you must use the built-in Mail app on iPhone. If you're using a third-party app like Gmail, Outlook or AOL Mail, you're missing out on Siri's smarts.

Keep in mind, even if you like using a dedicated third-party email app to manage your email, you can still add your email address to Apple's built-in app to get smarter Siri. We'll just turn off a few features so you don't get double notifications.

To start, go into **Settings > Accounts & Passwords**. If you don't see the email address you want to use in here, tap Add Account. If the email address you want to use is already listed here, I'll go over how to make sure the Siri feature is turned on after I explain how to add a new account.

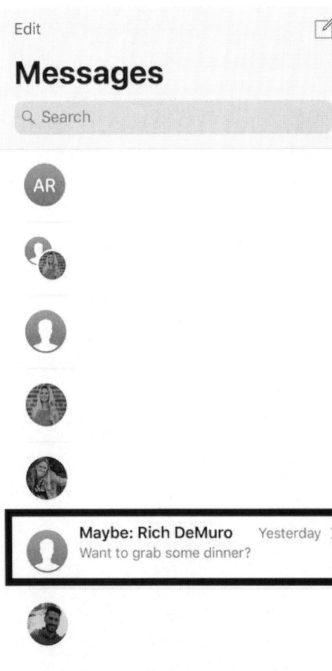

Have Siri identify people that aren't in your address book

Tap **Add Account**, then tap the logo of the account type you'd like to add.

Follow the steps to add your account, which usually involves inputting your email username and password. When that's all finished, you'll get a screen with some options to turn on various aspects of your account including Mail, Contacts, Calendars, Reminders and Notes. The only thing that must be turned on for Siri's smarts to work is Mail. The rest is up to you.

Press the **Save** button in the upper right-hand corner when you're finished.

Now, let's make sure the option is turned on for Siri to sort through our emails to look for contact information.

Go to **Settings** > **Mail** and look at the very top section labeled ALLOW MAIL TO ACCESS. The top option should be Siri & Search. Tap in here and make sure the slider shows that it's on (it should be green.) This allows Siri to look through the contents of your emails. Don't worry, Siri won't share them with anyone.

The second option labeled "Allow on Lock Screen" allows Siri to surface suggestions on your lock screen. I'd leave this one turned on as well.

Now, go to **Settings** > **Contacts** and look in the top section labeled ALLOW CONTACTS TO ACCESS and the top option should be Siri & Search.

Tap here and look for the toggles for **Siri & Suggestions**, **Allow on Lock Screen** as well as **Find Contacts in Other Apps**. Be sure that these options are turned on.

From now on, when you get an email, Siri will scan it for

any information she can use to tell you more about the people contacting you.

For example, you might see Siri's suggestions about who a person is when someone calls, texts or emails you.

My favorite way to use this data?

The pull-down!

You will quickly realize adding contacts to your address book is almost unnecessary with Siri on your side.

Siri always seems to have the latest data on your contacts.

Try it: Pull down on your home screen to bring up the Siri Search bar and type in the name of someone that you know isn't in your address book but you've probably exchanged an email with before.

You'll see them pop up in a section labeled SIRI FOUND IN MAIL.

To me, this is a really useful feature since I'm often working with contacts at a company on a TV segment that I've exchanged a bunch of emails with but I don't necessarily need them in my address book forever.

However, if you do want to add this person's information or update their contact info in your address book, there are options to do that too once you tap their name.

When I need to get in touch with someone fast, I can just use Siri Search to lookup their name and see if she's captured data from their signature line.

If you want to help out the folks you do business with, include pertinent information in your email signatures like your Name, address, phone number and email address so Siri can find you!

Now, remember I said you can use this feature even if you

don't want to use the built-in Mail app on iPhone. You might notice as soon as you connect an email account to the app your phone starts buzzing and making a sound every time you get new mail.

To turn this off, go to **Settings** > **Mail** > **Notifications**. Then just tap the toggle to turn off notifications for the Mail app. Your mail will still be fetched and searched by Siri, but this will all happen in the background. If you have multiple email accounts, just tap the email account you want to silence and set the Vibration to None and the ALERT TONES to None.

86

Respond fast with canned phrases

We're all guilty of this – our phone rings while we're busy, we pick it up and say "I can't talk right now, can I call you back?"

Wouldn't it be nicer to just respond instantly with a text?

That's exactly what the iPhone lets you do.

Next time, take a closer look at your incoming call screen. In addition to the typical pickup and hangup buttons, there is another helpful option.

It's a button that says **Message**.

It sits right above the button to accept a call. Press it and you can instantly send a pre-written text message to the person that's calling you.

‹ Phone   **Respond with Text**

RESPOND WITH:

I'm on the air right now. can I call u back in 5?   ⊗

I'm on my way.

Can I call you later?

These quick responses will be available when you
respond to an incoming call with a text. Change them to
say anything you like.

Customize your phrases to respond fast to calls you can't answer

iPhone has some built-in suggestions, but you can customize
them for your situation.

Canned responses from the factory are:

- *Sorry, I can't talk right now.*

- *I'm on my way.*

- *Can I call you later?*

But you can change these to anything you like!

For me, mine might be more like:

- *I'm on TV right now, can I call you back in 5 minutes.*

- *Is everything OK?*

- *In a meeting, will call you back later.*

Or you can even put things like:

- *Can you call me on my office line at 310-555-1212?*

- *Email me at hello@richontech.tv, I respond faster*

- *Don't leave a voicemail, I never check it anyway*

To customize these options to something that works for you, head into **Settings** > **Phone** > **Respond with Text**.

You'll see three lines you can customize with your personal messages.

Just tap a line and type in whatever you want!

The next time someone calls your phone, instead of declining the call, just hit the **Message** button on the incoming call screen.

You'll see your three custom canned responses along with a fourth option to type a one-time custom message.

As soon as you choose an option, your incoming call will be declined, sent to voicemail and your text sent to the caller immediately!

It's a simple feature that can save you a game of phone tag or at the least, a check of your voicemail.

87

Quickly scan a document into a PDF and sign it too

Need to scan and or sign a document fast? Look no further than the Notes app on the iPhone.

A recent update makes it super easy to convert a printed page digital and even add notes or your signature.

To scan a piece of paper, just open up the Notes app and press the option to start a fresh note. This is the icon in the lower right-hand corner that looks like a little box with a pen on it.

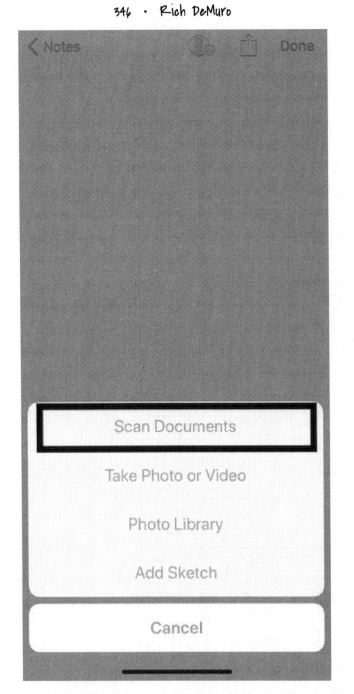

Easily scan documents with a feature built into Notes

On the next screen, look for a little strip of icons above the keyboard. Tap the one that has a circle with a plus sign in it.

This will bring up a menu with an option to **Scan Documents**.

Tap it and your phone instantly turns into a document scanner!

This can be useful for many reasons.

You can scan paper bills to digitally archive them, you can scan expense report receipts while you're still on the road so you don't lose them, scan in your kids' artwork and more.

To scan a document, just hold your phone over the item you want to scan.

In this mode, the iPhone camera will automatically recognize the edges of the document you are scanning, highlight them in yellow, and then automatically scan, crop and straighten your item.

Contrasting colors work best – so if your receipt is white, place it on a dark surface so the software can properly detect the edges.

You can keep scanning additional pages until you're finished.

Need to go back and delete a page – just tap the little stack of completed scans in the left-hand corner of your screen, right next to the shutter button.

When you're finished with your scans, you can tap the button in the lower right-hand corner to save your documents.

Once a **Scanned Document** is inside a note, you can tap it to make changes. You'll see a row of icons at the bottom to add additional scans, crop the document and switch the capture style between Color, Grayscale, Black & White or Photo. You can also manually rotate your scan or trash it all together.

At this point, you can just store the document in notes, send it off to another app for safekeeping, or email the scan to someone else.

One thing to know about this – what you send depends on the screen you do it from.

For instance, if you are in a note and tap the share button, which is located in the upper right-hand corner of your screen, you will share the entire note, along with the scanned documents inside.

If you want to share just the scanned documents themselves, for example, as a PDF file, you will want to first go into a note with the documents, then tap the documents, THEN press the share button. This is the cleaner way to share just the documents inside the note, but there might be occasions when you want to share the entire note, along with whatever attachments are inside.

If you want to add drawings, circles, text or your signature to your scanned document, go into a note containing a document, then tap on the Scanned Documents inside.

Now, hit the share button and look along the bottom row for an option labeled Markup.

This will bring up your markup tools.

You can draw, highlight and add shapes. If you want to add text or your signature, just hit the plus sign in the circle at the far right.

It's a little confusing to have the Markup tools located in such a hidden place, perhaps Apple will move them more out in the open in a future software update.

Keep in mind, when you sign a document, your iPhone will save your signature for next time. If you don't want your signature stored in your phone, just use the option to Add or Remove signature to delete it from your device.

Now, scan away!

88

Share a to do list

One of the handiest things I've done around the house was not an item on my To Do list, but actually sharing that To Do list with my wife.

The reason? We're both on the same page when it comes to what we need to get done.

Sharing a list in the Reminders app is a super easy way to exchange quick little bits of information with your significant other, a colleague or anyone else with an iPhone.

My wife and I tried the family to-do list but that didn't work out too well. She kept adding things and I kept feeling more and more guilty that they weren't done.

But one list we've shared that really comes in handy is a shopping list. I know, super basic, but we can add things to the list when we run out of something, and more importantly, we can sit down and make a shopping list together and then whoever goes to the store can just cross off each item as it's purchased.

To start, open the **Reminders** app. You can use the built-in To Do list or you can create a new one to share. For the purposes of my example, I will create a new list and share that.

To make a new list, drag down from the top of your screen in the section where it says the title of the current list you're viewing. If your list says To Do, just drag down from there until you see a search bar and plus sign appear at the top of your screen.

Now, tap the + sign and choose the option to create a new list.

Give your list a name – let's call it **Shopping List** – and use the dots below to choose a color for the list.

Hit **Done** when you're finished.

Now you should have a list titled Shopping List with nothing in it. Before you start to add all of the groceries you need, tap the Edit button under the number in the upper right-hand corner of the list.

This brings up two new options – **Color** and **Sharing**. We already chose a color for our list title, but if you want to change it, now you know where to go.

We're going to tap the second option labeled **Sharing**.

From here, tap the option to **Add person...** and you can now start typing the name of the person you want to share the list with. Just make sure the person you are sharing with has their email or phone number associated with an iCloud account.

Tap **Add** when you're finished and the person you're attempting to share the list with will get a notification on their device that you would like to share the list with them. If they don't see the notification right away, have them open the Reminders app and look in there.

Your recipient has the option to **Decline** or **Accept** your invitation to share the list. Once they tap **Accept**, you'll get a notification that that person has joined your shared reminders list.

Once you're finished sharing, press the + sign to add an item to the list. You should see whatever you write immediately show up on the list displayed on their device too!

Now, try tapping the circle next to one of the items in the list to mark it complete. You'll see it disappear on both screens. If it's still displayed, but with a full circle next to it, just tap the bottom of the screen where it says **Show Completed** / **Hide Completed**. Toggle that a few times to see the difference. Some people like to see a completed list, others (like myself) like items to disappear from the list once they've been virtually crossed off. It's up to you!

At this point, either of you can add or delete items to the list you've shared and the information will be synced between your devices.

If you no longer want to share the list with the other person, just tap **Edit** once again, then **Sharing**. This should reveal a list of all of the people you're sharing the list with. Just swipe from right to left on the person that you want to delete to reveal a **Stop Sharing** button. Tap here to remove the person from the list.

Your grocery store trips will be so efficient from here on out – while you're there, can you grab me some of those sparkling waters everyone is crazy about? Thanks.

89

Have a reminder trigger at a time or location

Reminders is a powerful little app on the iPhone. You can have multiple lists to help you complete your tasks or, if you're like me, put an item on your To Do list to ensure that it never gets done!

You can use Siri to create a reminder – Hey Siri, Remind me to… – or just type it in.

Once a reminder is created, there are some things we can do to them to make them even more useful.

For starters, 3D Touch on a reminder you've already made.

You'll see two options pop up: "Remind me on a day" and "Remind me at a location." Both can be incredibly handy for making a reminder work harder for you.

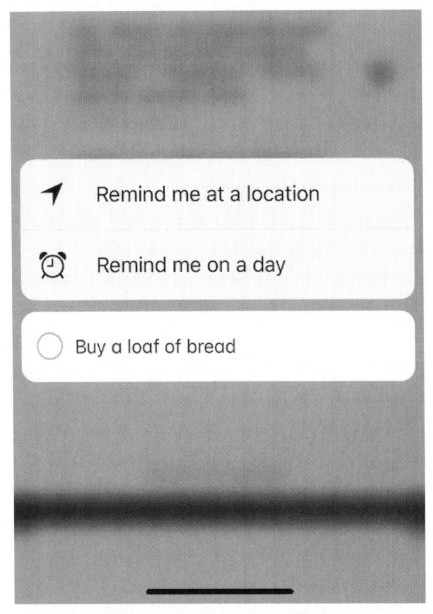

3D Touch a reminder to have it trigger at a time or location

The first, **Remind me on a day**, is pretty easy to understand. Tap to edit the date and time you'll be reminded of something.

You can even have it repeat. This can be super useful for reminding you to take your medication at a certain time, taking the trash cans out each week or writing a recurring check to someone.

Remind me at a location can be even more powerful. Tap this option to bring up a search box where you can input a location for your reminder to pop up.

Your iPhone might even suggest some frequent locations or even an action, like **Getting in the car** or **Getting out of the car**.

You can also search for any location you want and have your reminder pop up the next time you visit that location.

For example, let's say you need more laundry detergent. You can set a reminder for more detergent to trigger when you step into your preferred grocery store. Or maybe there's something you only buy at Target since it's cheaper there. You can set a reminder to trigger when you go to Target. Just search for the name of the place then select the proper location from the list.

Alternatively, you can say something like "Hey Siri, remind me to buy laundry detergent the next time I'm at Target." Siri should respond with a list of matching businesses so you can select the one you'd like your reminder to pop up at.

It's super easy to set up a recurring reminder with Siri. Just say something like "Hey Siri, remind me to fill out my time card every Friday at 8 AM" or "Hey Siri, remind me to take out the trash cans when I get home on Thursdays."

One more note about the reminders you've created. You probably already know that you can tap the little circle next to them to mark them as completed, but if you would rather delete them entirely, just swipe on a reminder from right to left. You'll also get a **More** option which can be used to edit the details of a reminder.

90

Set a specific ring or text tone for a contact

It's pretty crazy how identifiable the default iPhone ringtone is. You hear it all day long in the office. Out and about at the mall. And in movies. So many of us don't even bother to change the default ringtones or notification tones that ship with the phone.

I'm guilty of it.

Even if you don't bother to change the main ring and message tones, here's a way to set specific tones for certain contacts so you know who's getting in touch with you just by hearing their unique sound.

First, go to your **Contacts**. You can do this through the Phone app or just open the Contacts app.

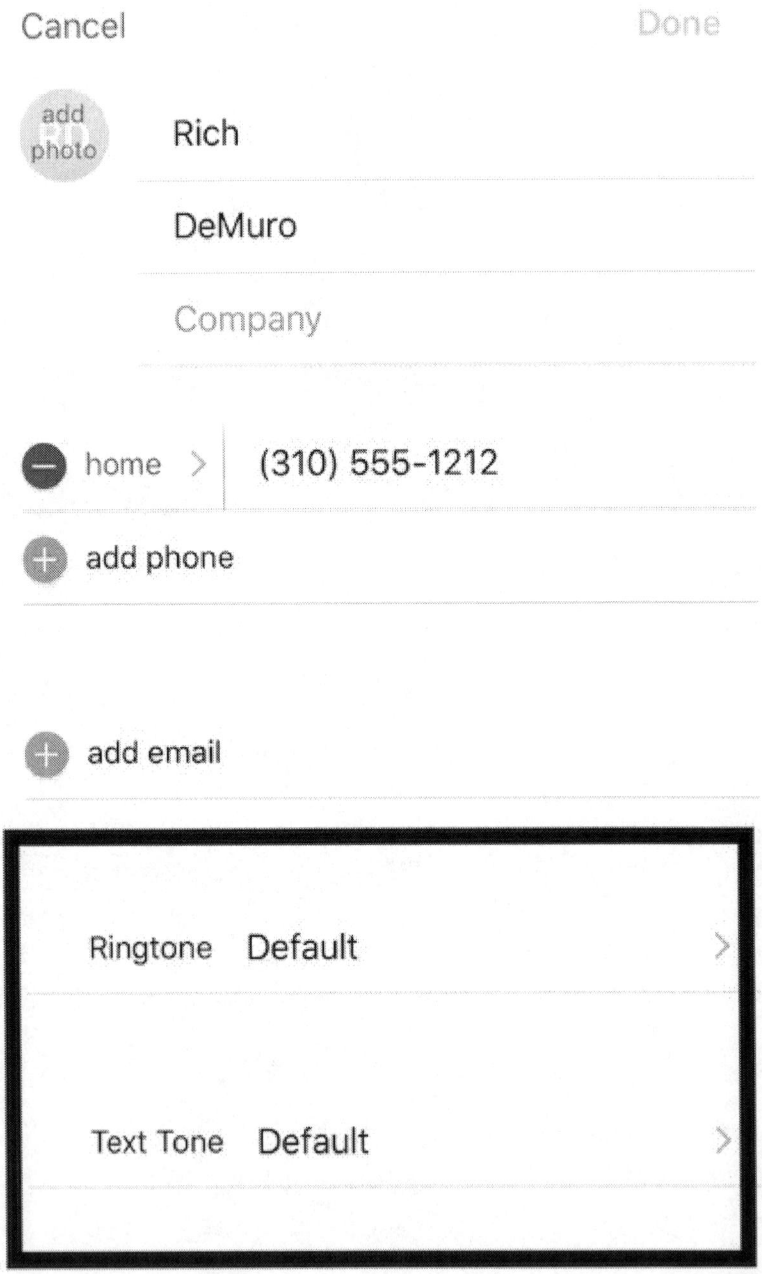

Cancel   Done

add
photo   Rich

             DeMuro

             Company

⊖ home >   (310) 555-1212

⊕ add phone

⊕ add email

Ringtone   Default   >

Text Tone   Default   >

Easily identify who's calling by assigning a specific ringtone

Now, select a contact you'd like to customize with a particular Ringtone or Text Tone.

Tap their name, then hit the **Edit** button in the upper right-hand corner of the screen.

Look for the section that says **Ringtone** and **Text Tone**. Most likely, they say Default.

If you want to change their Ringtone, tap that section and it will bring you to a bunch of options. You can buy a new ringtone from the Tone Store, select from your previously purchased Ringtones (you might have to hit the option to Download All Purchased Tones first) or just scroll to the areas that have the RINGTONES and ALERT TONES preinstalled on your phone.

Tap a sound to hear a preview. Tap again to stop the preview. Keep in mind you can select audio from both RINGTONES and ALERT TONES for incoming calls from this contact. RINGTONES are generally longer and more melodious, while ALERT TONES are just a few short notes.

While you're on this screen, there are a few other things you do to customize your selected contact. At the top is an option called **Emergency Bypass**, which sounds like a surgery, but it lets this contact's calls come through even if you have **Do Not Disturb** enabled. See the tip for setting up Do Not Disturb for more on this feature.

Under Emergency Bypass, there's an option to change the **Vibration** for the selected contact. You can choose from a selection of pre-programmed vibrations or even create your own custom vibration!

When you're finished, hit the Done button in the upper right-hand corner of your screen.

If you'd like to change their Text Tone, you can do it now.

While still in the Edit screen of your contact, hit the option for Text Tone. Again, you'll see options to choose a Tone from the store, an ALERT TONE from the list of pre-installed options or even a RINGTONE. Notice the ALERT TONES and RINGTONES are swapped this time? You're free to choose a RINGTONE for an incoming text, but be prepared to deal with the repercussions of really long notifications when someone messages you a simple "What's Up?."

Be sure to hit done when you're finished selecting your new sounds.

Once you've finished customizing your contact, hit Done once again to save these changes to your contact. Now when they call, you will hear a special sound you can identify instantly.

91

Backup and sync your texts across multiple devices

While you might be under the impression that your messages on the iPhone are saved and synced across your various devices, up until now that's only been partly true.

It's true that iCloud backs up your messages so when you get a new phone you have likely seen old texts appear on your new device.

It's also true that the **Messages** app has the ability to deliver your messages to your various devices.

But if you took a real close look at the state of affairs when it comes to your messages, you would realize that they were not truly synced across all of your Apple devices, at least not until now.

A relatively new feature called **Messages in iCloud** finally syncs your messages across all of your Apple devices. It can also free up valuable storage space on your iPhone.

On the flip side, it will likely take up a bit more of your iCloud storage space. I'll explain why that is in a bit.

This can be a powerful feature, especially if you check your messages on multiple devices, like an iPhone and iPad or an iPhone and Mac Computer.

Once you turn it on, all the messages you receive on your phone – SMS and iMessages – will appear on all of your devices. Additionally, when you delete a message on one device and it will now be gone from the others.

To set up Messages in iCloud, you'll need to have the latest version of iOS installed on your iPhone or iPad.

Go to **Settings** > **General** > **Software Update** and be sure you're up to date.

Before we turn the feature on, let me explain how Messages in iCloud can free up valuable storage space on your phone.

With Messages in iCloud, photos and attachments in your messages, as well as your older texts are actually stored in iCloud, so this frees up local storage space on your phone. Your device will still display all of your messages and their contents as normal, but some of the information will be pulled from the cloud on demand – only when you tap to access it.

But the best part about all of this is that when you get a new device, it will be restored with all of your messages, not just the ones you had on the device you restored your backup from.

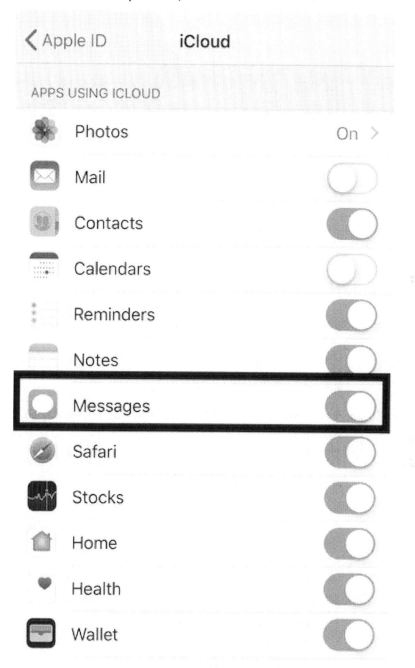

Turn on Messages in iCloud for backup and sync across all of your devices

To set up Messages in iCloud, make sure the software on your phone is up to date. If it isn't, you won't see the next option we're going to turn on.

Next, go to **Settings**, then tap your name at the top of the list, the one that says Apple ID, iCloud, iTunes & App Store under it.

On the next screen, tap **iCloud**.

You should now see a list of APPS USING ICLOUD. Look for **Messages** in the list and tap the toggle next to it so it turns green, which means it's on.

At this point, if you don't have Two Factor Authentication turned on, Apple will walk you through the process to do that before you can enable Messages in iCloud. This is for your security since Messages often contain sensitive personal information and Apple wants to make sure your account is as locked down as possible.

From here on out, every time you log in with your Apple ID, you'll get a notification or text message with a special code that must be entered before the login can proceed. It's an extra step but more secure. See the tip on Two Factor Authentication for more on how that feature can protect your account.

Once you successfully enable Messages in iCloud, your iPhone will upload all of your messages to iCloud and safely store them there. Next time you upgrade to a new device or add an additional device to your account and activate Messages in iCloud on it, you'll have the exact same list of messages everywhere. Whatever changes you make on one device will be reflected on the others.

If you have another iPhone or iPad you'd like to sync up, just follow the same steps to turn on Messages in iCloud.

If you have a Mac computer, you can turn on Messages in iCloud by opening the Messages app and going to the menu bar and clicking **Messages > Preferences**. Look for the option under your Apple ID to "Enable Messages in iCloud."

Just like your phone, you will need a newer version of Apple's desktop software to enable this feature, which is anything 10.13.5 and higher.

Now the flip side of all of this: Messages in iCloud will take up more of your iCloud storage. That's because all of your messages will now be stored online, but I think the benefit of having all of your messages synced across multiple devices is a small price to pay.

Keep in mind you only get 5 gigabytes of free iCloud storage so between your photos and messages you might need to pay a little more each month to have everything backed up online.

92

Scan a QR code

At some point in your life, you've probably come across a strange looking square that seems like it's some sort of barcode from the future. It is, but they've been around for a while now. It's called a QR code and it's a handy way to get more information about something instantly.

Your iPhone can help you recognize these little codes in seconds, and reveal the information hidden behind them.

Think of a QR code like a barcode they scan at checkout, but instead of ringing up the price, it can contain little bits of information like a web address, contact card and more.

For some reason, QR codes haven't taken off as rapidly here in the United States, but they are very popular in Asia. It's probably since people scan QR codes on each other's phones to link up in social media apps. It's much faster than trying to search for someone's username.

Anyway, there are a few ways to scan a QR code on your iPhone.

The simplest way is to just aim your iPhone camera at one of the codes. It will instantly recognize it!

In fact, you don't even need to hit the shutter button. If you do, it won't work!

You probably didn't realize this, but your iPhone camera is constantly performing calculations from the moment you start opening the app. It's looking for cues like light or dark, person or animal and landscape or flower. In the process, it will recognize QR codes.

You can try this by scanning the code below with your iPhone.

Just open the camera and aim it at the code so you can see it on your screen.

Within seconds, you'll see a little pop up on your screen that says something to the effect of WEBSITE QR CODE and "Open "richontech.tv in Safari."

Your iPhone has decoded the QR code and fetched a little preview of the information it contains. If you tap the notification banner, it will take you right to the page that is programmed into the QR code. Keep in mind your phone needs to be connected to the internet for this to happen. Otherwise, it can't decode the QR code.

Alternatively, if you want a little preview of the information the QR code contains, you can pull down on the notification. It might show you a website, contact information or something else. If you want to proceed, you can tap the button below the preview.

There are a few other ways to scan a QR code with your iPhone. If you have an iPhone with 3D Touch, you can 3D Touch the Camera icon. This will bring up several options including one to Scan QR Code.

You can also add a button to scan QR codes in your Control Center. Just go to **Settings** > **Control Center** > **Customize Controls** and tap the plus sign next to **Scan QR Code**. Now, when you access your Control Center you will see a little button with a QR code on it. Tap it to scan a code.

The funny part about both of these shortcuts is that you really don't need them. In the end, all you really need to do is aim your iPhone camera at a QR code and it will go to work to decode it.

That is, unless you don't like the idea of your phone

automatically scanning codes. In this case, you can turn off the QR code recognition by going into **Settings** > **Camera** and toggling the switch next to "Scan QR Codes." Now, to scan a code you will have to activate the feature first by using the Control Center button or the 3D Touch option.

PART XI

Wellness

93

Wake up to a gradual alarm

There's nothing gradual about the iPhone alarm as a means to wake up. It is jarring and in your face.

That's because unlike just about every other phone I've tested, iPhone alarms don't have a setting that lets them gradually increase the volume.

Personally, I like to ease into my day as peacefully as possible.

Thankfully, there's a feature called Bedtime that can help you get a more gradual wake up call.

You'll find **Bedtime** in the **Clock** app.

Once you open the app, look in the bottom row for a section called Bedtime and tap it.

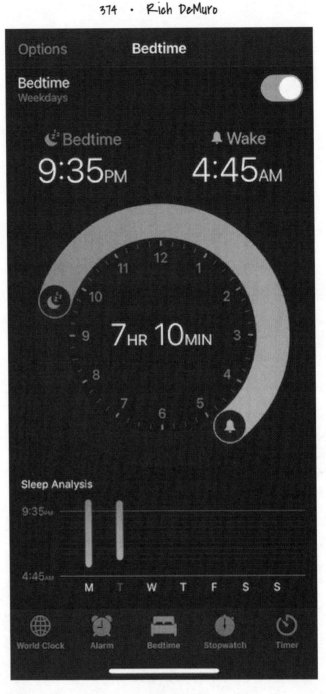

Wake up to gradual alarm clock by using Bedtime

You'll see a circular clock type slider in the middle of the screen, along with a **Bedtime** and **Wake** time. Apple built this feature as a way to help you get to bed on time, but the nice thing is that the **Wake Up Sounds** start soft and gradually get louder.

To set it up, move the slider with the moon on it to the time you'd ideally go to bed each night. Then, move the slider with the bell on it to the time you would like your morning alarm to go off (gradually!).

Notice something? You can only adjust the sleep and wake up times in 5-minute intervals. In the middle of the clock, you'll see the estimated amount of sleep you'll get with these settings.

Now, look near the upper left-hand corner of the screen and tap **Options**.

Here, you can adjust all of your settings including the wake-up sound and volume, as well as the days of the week for your alarm to go off.

Tap where it says **Bedtime Reminder** for another useful feature, especially if you're a binge watcher and frequently lose track of time at night. Turn this on and your iPhone will send you a notification when it's getting near the time you should go to sleep for a good night's sleep.

You'll love the sound of this Bedtime reminder notification – I promise.

Want to hear what your gradual alarm will sound like?

Just tap where it says **Wake Up Sound** and you'll see your (somewhat limited) options to choose from. Select one and you'll notice that it starts out nice and soft and eventually gets louder.

You can also have your phone vibrate while the sound goes off as well.

Back out to save your choices.

One more option on the main screen to turn on is the **Do Not Disturb During Bedtime**, which is new for iOS 12. This will put your phone into Bedtime mode for the duration you chose on the previous screen. This means your lock screen will be dimmed, it won't show notifications on the main screen (you can still find them by the normal swipe down if you unlock your phone) and calls and alerts will be silenced.

Calls and text from important contacts you set up in Do Not Disturb will still ring through.

When you're done with all of your options, hit **Done** and you'll be taken to the main screen. If you wake up at the same time each day, you don't have to do much more. But if you wake up at different times on different days, you'll have to adjust the Wake side of the slider before you go to sleep. Don't forget!

One more thing – if you're concerned that the more gentle sound won't wake you up, you can do what I do. Set a backup alarm. Just use the standard Alarm section at the bottom of the screen to set a regular Alarm as you did in the past. I usually set mine for 5 minutes after my Bedtime wakeup sound.

If I wake up on time, then I just turn off the second alarm before it rings.

Now, enjoy your more peaceful mornings. Unless you have little kids, then you probably don't need an alarm clock anyway.

94

See your step count

You might think that you need a fancy fitness tracker or an Apple Watch to see how far you've walked in a day or how many flights of stairs you've climbed, but you can get some of this data right from built-in sensors on your iPhone.

It all starts with the Health app. If you haven't opened it yet, the first time you do you'll get a prompt to fill out some information about yourself. Input whatever you're comfortable sharing with the app.

From now on, your phone will track things like how many steps you take, the floors you climb and more.

Keep in mind, since your phone is collecting this data from onboard sensors, it might not be as accurate as wearing an actual fitness tracker.

See your step count in the Health app

You can see your progress by opening the **Health** App and tapping the **Today** tab at the bottom.

Immediately, you should see a bunch of data along with today's date. If you want to go to another day's data, just tap another date up at the top, or explore the entire calendar.

When you want to go back to today's data, use tap the Today tab at the bottom of the screen once again.

To dive a little deeper into the data, just tap one of the **Activity** bars. Tap **Steps** to see a bar chart with your steps plotted by the hour.

Tap the D, W, M or Y at the top of the chart to see our averages for those time frames.

If you want to see a particular measurement on your Today screen more prominently, just toggle the little switch next to **Add to Favorites**.

On this screen, there is also an option to **Show All Data**. Tap here to see a day by day count of each day's recorded data, and you can even drill in further to see exactly where this data came from. Tap the date to get an even bigger breakdown of the blocks of data by that date. And if you're really data hungry, tap one more time to see specific details of the device that reported that data, including the name, manufacturer, hardware version and software version. This could come in handy if you're troubleshooting something that doesn't look right.

Back on the screen with the bar chart, you'll notice under Show All Data, there's an option for **Data Sources & Access**. Tap here to see a list of all of the DATA SOURCES for a given metric. This could include devices AND apps. For instance, if you wear an Apple Watch it is also counting your steps.

Additionally, any fitness apps you might use to workout could also report information back into here. You'll see a list of everything that is reporting to your totals.

You can also re-arrange your DATA SOURCES to prioritize a certain device. Let's say you carry a work iPhone, a personal iPhone and wear an Apple Watch all day. At night when you go out you only bring your personal iPhone. You can pre-order your data sources so they are in the priority you want: Apple Watch, personal iPhone, work iPhone. This way you get the best tracking out of your devices that are on you most. Tap the **Edit** button in the upper right-hand corner to rearrange your sources.

If you are confused as to why a certain app or device is contributing to your Health data, tap the Sources tab at the bottom of the screen. This will show you a list of all of the APPS and DEVICES that can contribute data to your totals.

If you see a device you no longer use or an app you don't want tracking you, you can get rid of it.

For APPS, tap the app you no longer want contributing and you'll have options to either **Delete All Data** or **Turn All Categories Off or On**.

As for devices, tap a device to see the ACTIVITY it can contribute and if you no longer need the device or it's data, tap **Delete All Data** from [device name]. You'll get a confirmation that the data associated with that device will be deleted permanently.

You really don't have to play with any or all of these settings, I'm just letting you know that they're there. There might come a time when you wonder why "mindfulness minutes" pop up on your Health Activity dashboard and how your phone knew you were meditating during that time. It's all because a connected app was reporting back to the Health App.

Knowing this information is here can be helpful for whatever healthy lifestyle goals you're working towards.

PART XII

Surfing the Web

95

Close all of your open tabs instantly

If you've used your iPhone for a while, chances are you've got a bunch of web pages open in the background and don't even know it! This is one of the most popular tips I've ever shared on TV – I got emails, Tweets and messages for days from folks telling me how many pages they closed out with this little trick.

Often, when you do a search or open a link on Safari, it's actually opening in what's called a "new tab." Theoretically, this makes it easy for you to go back to that page and have multiple pages open at once for easy reference, but in reality, lots of people forget these multiple tabs are open.

First, we'll take a look at all of our open tabs then I'll show you how to close them all out at once – it might be the most satisfying move you'll ever make on your iPhone.

Open **Safari**. You should see a strip at the bottom of the page with several options – the one closest to the bottom right corner looks like two little boxes on top of each other.

Tap here and you will see a new screen with all of your open tabs. If you're super tidy, you might see just one. If you haven't tapped those two boxes in a while, you might see a bunch of old websites you've visited in the past. You can even try scrolling through them with your finger to take a walk through your Internet history past. Tapping on a page brings it full screen.

You'll notice in the left-hand corner of each floating page there is a little X. If you tap it, you can clear this page out. Alternatively, you can swipe a page from right to left to clear it out and send it away. Pretty simple if you have just a few pages to deal with.

But the most fun way to clear out all of these lingering tabs is with a shortcut.

On the screen with the floating web pages, instead of tapping the **Done** button once, tap and hold it. You'll get a new option to close out all of your tabs at once. Take a look at the number you get – people have told me it has been in the hundreds!

One more confirmation tap on the "Close All Tabs" and they will all go away.

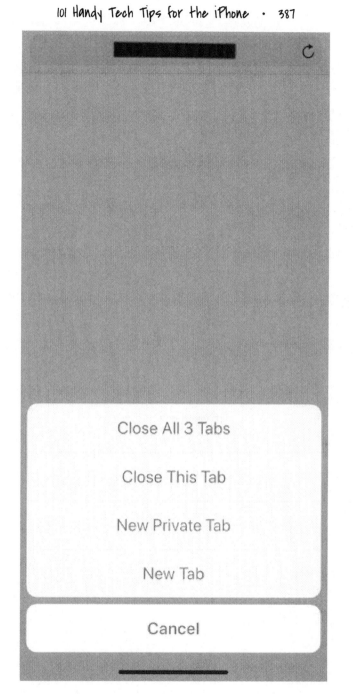

Close out all of your old tabs at once

You can also accomplish this from the main Safari screen.

Go back to a screen where you can see the overlapping boxes icon, and instead of tapping it, press it hard, or press and hold it for a second.

You'll get a new list of options, including **Close Tabs, Close This Tab, New Private Tab** and **New Tab**.

You know what to do. Just hit **Close Tabs** and they will all go away.

There you have it, several ways to clear out your lingering web pages.

Once you know this little trick you might be using it a lot depending on your preferred level of neatness. There are two types of people in this world – those that don't mind a million different tabs open, and those that do.

Bet you didn't know which one you were until just now.

96

Read an article without on screen distractions

Reading articles online isn't always easy. Between the ads, auto-playing videos and everything else littering the screen, it can be distracting. Thankfully, Safari has a handy little way to focus in on just the article text on a web page so you can concentrate on reading.

First, open **Safari** on your iPhone and find an article you'd like to read. The more distractions on the page, the better.

Now, look in the upper left-hand corner of the screen. You should see **four little lines** with the bottom one shorter than the others. It is to the left of the address bar, which contains the web address of the page you're visiting.

If you don't see it, scroll back to the top of the page.

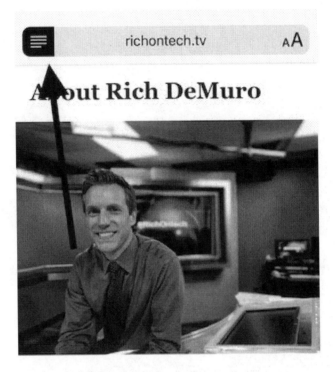

richontech.tv ᴀA

About Rich DeMuro

Rich DeMuro is the tech reporter for KTLA-TV Channel 5 in Los Angeles and appears on the #1 rated KTLA Morning News. Viewers around the nation know him as "Rich on Tech" and his segment is syndicated on dozens of Tribune TV stations. Every week, Rich shares tech news, tips and gadget reviews with news programs in New York, Chicago, San Francisco, New Orleans, Indianapolis, San

Tap the little lines for a distraction-free view of an article

Now, tap those little lines.

Immediately, you'll notice that your page reformats to include just the main parts including the article text and any photos. Tap the icon a few times to compare the differences. A lot less distracting, right?

Apple calls this **Reader View**, and it's a much more pleasant way of reading online articles.

When you're in Reader View, you'll notice a new option to the right of the web page address at the top of the screen: two letters, a little A and a big A.

Tap here to customize your view options. You can change the font, background color of the page and the size of the text.

My favorites are Georgia and a Sepia toned background. Reminds me of a good old-fashioned book.

Go to another article, hit the Reader View icon and you'll notice your preferences are saved.

Normally, you'll have to manually activate Reader View on every article you want to see that way. But there is also a way to make Safari remember your preferences for a particular website or even all websites.

This time, navigate to an article and long press the Reader View icon. You'll now see a special menu pop up titled Automatic Reader View.

You can use these options to look at all of the articles on a website in Reader View, or on all websites in general.

Safari even knows the difference between the home page of a website and an article.

If you change your mind, you can always go back to an article, long press the Reader Review icon, and choose the option to "Stop Using" on the website.

But I have a feeling once you discover the crisp, clean power of Reader View, you might not go back to that cluttered, distracted view.

You might almost feel sorry for the ads you'll miss.

97

Save an article to read later

We come across so many interesting articles to read on the web each and every day. Problem is, we might not have the time to sit back and read a particular article the instant we find it.

That's why there is a feature on the iPhone that lets you save the interesting articles you come across on a daily basis. This way you can read them later when you have the time, and maybe a nice cup of coffee.

The feature is called **Reading List**. You can find it by opening Safari and tapping what looks like the icon for an open book at the bottom of the screen, then tapping the icon for the eyeglasses.

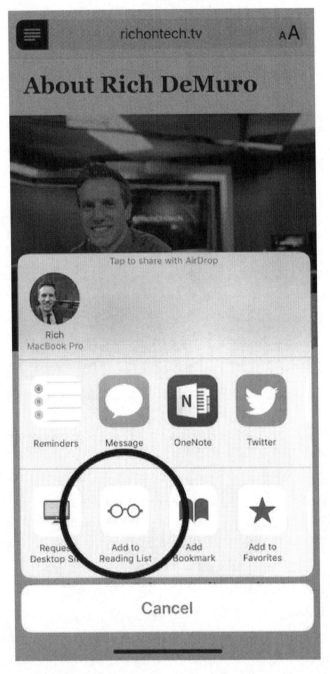

Add an article to your Reading List to enjoy later

This is your Reading List, and it could be empty, or perhaps you might find an article you've already earmarked to read later.

Let me show you how to save items in here.

Close out of your reading list, then navigate to an article on the web you'd like to read later.

Now, tap the little share icon at the bottom of the screen – it's the one that looks like a box with a little arrow coming out it.

This will bring up your **Share Sheet**, or all the ways you can share from your iPhone. Look for an icon on the bottom row labeled **Add to Reading List**.

Tap here and the article on your screen will be saved for later.

How's this different from a bookmark, you ask?

Let's take a look.

Remember that little icon that looks like a book? Let's go in there again and bring up our Reading List. You should see the article you just added at the top.

When you're done reading some items on your list, you can just swipe left on an item to bring up the option to delete it from your list.

A few more tricks to know about the reading list. First, your iPhone can save a copy of these articles so you can read them even when your phone isn't connected to the internet, like when you're on a plane.

To set this up, go into **Settings** > **Safari** and scroll down to where you see the section labeled READING LIST. Turn on the toggle for "Automatically Save Offline." If it's green, your iPhone will attempt to save a copy of the article to your phone.

Keep in mind this doesn't work with all websites. Some of them prevent the feature from working properly.

Now, let's go back to the Reading List screen. There are several more options to explore. The first is in the lower left-hand corner where it says Show Unread. Tap here to see just the articles you haven't read yet.

Again, you can also delete articles out of your Reading List by **swiping right to left** on one and tapping the **Delete** button that appears.

But, you might not want to do this because there is one more hidden feature in the Reading List, and that's the ability to search for items. Just pull down on the Reading List to reveal a **Search Reading List** box. Type in a keyword here search the headlines of all of the articles you have marked to read later.

98

Open a Private Tab instantly

We're all pretty familiar with the fact that the web searches we do on our phone are stored in our browsing history. Sometimes, you might want to do a search that's better forgotten. Maybe you're checking up on an ex or an ailment you believe is about to be the end of you.

Perhaps it's a combination of both!

You'll want to use what's called a **Private Tab,** and there are several ways to open one up. Your iPhone doesn't keep a record of what you search on these pages.

There are several ways to open up a Private Tab.

The easiest is to just 3D Touch the Safari icon. This will bring up four options including one for **New Private Tab.**

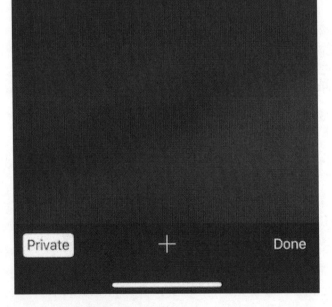

Private Browsing Mode

Tap it and you'll get a new web browsing tab.

Notice something different about it? It's dark grey around the top and bottom edges. This signifies that you are in a private browsing session.

The other way to open a Private Tab is from inside Safari itself. 3D Touch, the button in the lower right-hand corner that looks like two squares on top of each other. This will bring up options including **Close This Tab** or **New Private Tab**.

Tap the **New Private Tab** and again, you'll see the border around your browsing window change to a darker grey color, signifying you are in private mode.

You can also toggle Private mode by tapping those two little overlapping boxes once again. You'll see the word Private highlighted, along with a **Plus** sign and **Done**. Tapping Private will toggle you through your Private tabs and your regular web tabs.

One more thing to keep in mind. If you don't actually close out your Private Tab when you're finished using it, someone could come along and just hit the Private button we just used and bring up your Private Tabs and see exactly the sites you left behind.

If you don't want this to happen, be sure to enter Private mode and close out your tabs. You can do this by tapping the little X in the upper left hand corner of each tap, swiping on the tabs from right to left to delete them, or pressing and holding the Done button in the lower right hand corner to bring up the option to **Close All Tabs** or **Close This Tab** if it's your last one.

Just don't forget to go back to standard web browsing when you're done with your private browsing session.

I know this all sounds super confusing, and you might be wondering why you wouldn't want to just use Private mode all the time to minimize your browsing history.

This sounds good in theory but it could make things more complicated. For instance, you'll have to log into a website every time you visit it and if you need to go back to a page it will be tougher to find since it won't be in your history. Best to use Private browsing on a case by case basis.

Finally, a word about Private Tabs. Just because you're doing searches and browsing inside one doesn't mean that no one can see what you're looking at. Your Internet Service Provider, employer and others might still be able to see the sites you are browsing. The Private portion really refers to how Safari will "forget" what you were looking at as soon as you close out this particular tab.

If you don't close out your Tab at the end of your browsing session, someone could come along and just press the back button a bunch of times to see your entire browsing trail.

99

Find a word on a webpage

Finding a keyword on a webpage can really come in handy. Perhaps you're looking for the name of a character you love in a movie review, or the part you need to replace on an appliance.

Whatever the reason, there is a search function in Safari that can take you right to the keyword you need.

Problem is, the feature is totally hidden.

To find it, first, open up **Safari** and navigate to a web page, preferably an article.

Now, let's say you're reading an article about how to care for dogs and you want to get to the section where they talk about Dalmatians.

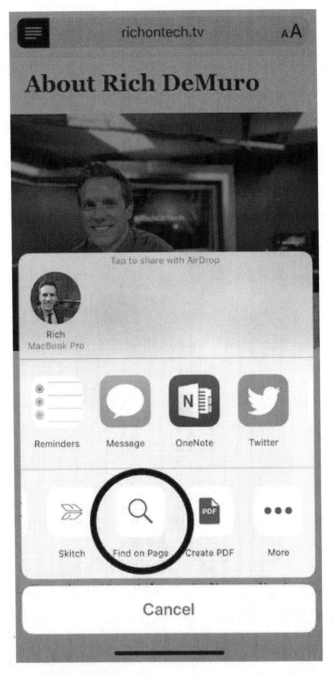

Search for a specific word on a webpage

At first glance, there doesn't seem to be a way to search the page for keywords, but the secret lies in the Share button at the bottom of the screen.

If you don't see it at first, just scroll up on the article or page a bit and a toolbar should appear at the bottom of your screen. Right in the center is a share button, which looks like a box with an arrow pointing out of it. Tap it and you'll see our handy share sheet.

Scroll through the icons on the bottom row until you see one labeled **Find on Page** with a magnifying glass. Tap it and a search box will pop up on your screen, just above your keyboard.

From here, type in the word you're looking for on the page. If it appears, Safari will immediately take you to that portion of the page and even highlight the word for you, or at least the characters of the word you've typed so far.

If the word appears more than once, you can use the little arrow keys to the left of the search box to find the next reference.

Want to search for something else? Just hit the little x next to the word you typed and you can try another search.

When you're finished, hit Done!

100

Request the desktop version of a website

When the iPhone first launched, a big part of how groundbreaking it was had to do with the fact that you could browse "real" versions of websites.

In the keynote and subsequent commercials, Apple would show how you could call up the New York Times website and see what you would see on a desktop screen, just smaller.

These days, websites usually have two versions – a desktop and a mobile-optimized site. This is fine for 99% of web browsing, but there are occasions when the mobile version of a website might not have the functionality you're looking for.

You might need to access the full "desktop" site to get it.

Try as you might, you can reload a page a bunch of times and still not get the "full site."

Thankfully, there is a way to have Safari "ask" the website to serve up a desktop version so you can get the full functionality, just in a smaller version on your phone screen.

Let's try it. Open **Safari** on your phone and go to a website like USAToday.com.

Notice how the website is "optimized" for your phone screen? Stories are displayed in a single column and there isn't much to the left or right of them since your phone doesn't have much screen real estate. It looks different than it would on your desktop, with a big screen to fill up.

Now, look at the bottom of your screen and right in the middle should be a **Share** icon – it looks like a little box with an arrow pointing up and out of it.

If you don't see it, just scroll down and back up the website a bit to reveal the menus at the top and bottom of your screen.

When you tap the share icon, it brings up the **Share Sheet**, with options to AirDrop, share to apps and system share functions on the bottom row. On that bottom row, look for an icon that's labeled **Request Desktop Site**. Tap it and the website will reload.

Request the desktop version of a website

Once the website is finished loading, it will look a lot more like the way it does on your desktop computer screen! The text is much smaller, the layout is no longer mobile optimized and all desktop functionality is intact.

You can pinch to zoom in or double tap on the screen to zoom all the way out again.

This Desktop version of a website can come in handy for various reasons, but mostly you won't know you need it until you are browsing the mobile version of a website and you realize you can't find a certain function – like a login screen or a tool you need. Now you know you can switch to the real thing in seconds.

Once you leave the website and come back, it will revert back to the mobile version.

Want another shortcut to load the desktop version of a website?

All you have to do is press and hold the "reload button" in the address bar at the top of your screen.

This is the part of your web browser that shows the URL or web address of the site you are on. The reload button is to the right and it looks like a little circle with an arrow going around.

Press and hold here until you get a message at the bottom of your screen that says **Request Desktop Site**. This will perform the same function as using the Share Sheet option.

Either way, now you know how to get to the full version of a website if you ever need it.

101

Organize what you see when you open a new tab

You probably open Safari on your iPhone multiple times a day – but have you ever actually taken a few seconds to set it up to work for you?

When you open a new tab, you might see some random favorites and another section called FREQUENTLY VISITED. Let's spend a few minutes to make this new page tab your own.

If you don't know how to see the new tab page, open **Safari** and tap the icon that looks like **two little squares** on top of each other in the lower right-hand corner.

From here, press the **plus** sign in the lower center of the screen and you'll get a brand new window.

The little icons you see at the top of the screen are your

favorites websites or bookmarks. You might have bookmarked some of these sites a long time ago and they could be pulled from Safari on your desktop or laptop computer, your iPad or an old iPhone. Apple syncs up all of these sources using iCloud. That's why these might be here when you haven't done anything with bookmarks in a long time.

If you'd like to add a site to your bookmarks, navigate to a website, then press the share icon at the bottom of your screen. From here, tap the option to Add Bookmark.

Now if we go back to a new tab page, you should see the page you just bookmarked.

To rearrange these little bookmark icons, lightly tap and hold one of them like you would an app icon on your home screen. Suddenly, you can pick it up and drag it to a new location. It's just like rearranging your apps. If you press too hard on the icon it will begin to open a preview of the webpage. Just a light tap and hold will do the trick.

You might notice when you tap and hold if you don't move the icon, you get two new options hovering above it: Delete and Edit. Delete will remove the bookmark while Edit lets you change its attributes. I usually like to abbreviate the website description to something shorter so it all fits under its tiny icon.

You can also create a new folder for groups of similar websites. Just tap in the box under LOCATION and hit **New Folder**. When you're finished, the new icon will be housed in a folder on the new tab page. Again, it all looks very similar to what you might do on your home screen.

See the section where it says FREQUENTLY VISITED? Is there an icon in there that you don't want there? Just lightly tap and hold on the icon. When you release your finger, you'll see a **Delete** button hovering over the icon. One more tap and the website is gone.

Alternatively, you can do all of these changes by using the bookmarks icon next at the bottom of the screen. It's an icon that looks like an open book. See what Apple did there? They're smart like that. Tap the icon to see your Bookmarks screen organized by Favorites, Bookmarks Menu and more. Tap into each category to see how they're arranged, and from here you can swipe right to left on a bookmark to bring up a delete button if you want to get rid of it.

You can also rearrange your bookmarks from this screen by tapping the **Edit** button in the lower right-hand corner. Just use the little grabber icon (three lines) that appears to the right of a bookmark press hard on it and drag the bookmarks in the order you would like them to appear on the new tab page.

Hit **Done** when you're finished, then **Done** again on the **Favorites** page to see your handiwork reflected on the New Tab page. Now, each time you open a new tab you'll feel so organized and proud of yourself.

Don't have any good bookmarks? I'd recommend a website called RichOnTech.tv. I hear it's pretty good.

PART XIII

Bonus Tip

Clear everything off of your phone

For all that it does, the iPhone is a pretty rock solid piece of software and hardware.

But there are times when you might need to give it a restart, or clear out some settings, or clear out everything so you can sell it or give it away to a friend.

There are several levels of reset – from a standard phone reset, to a light **Settings** reset, to a **Network Settings** reset, all the way up to the granddaddy of all resets (and my personal favorite) the **Erase All Content and Settings** reset.

I'm going to walk through each one and explain when you might need to use it.

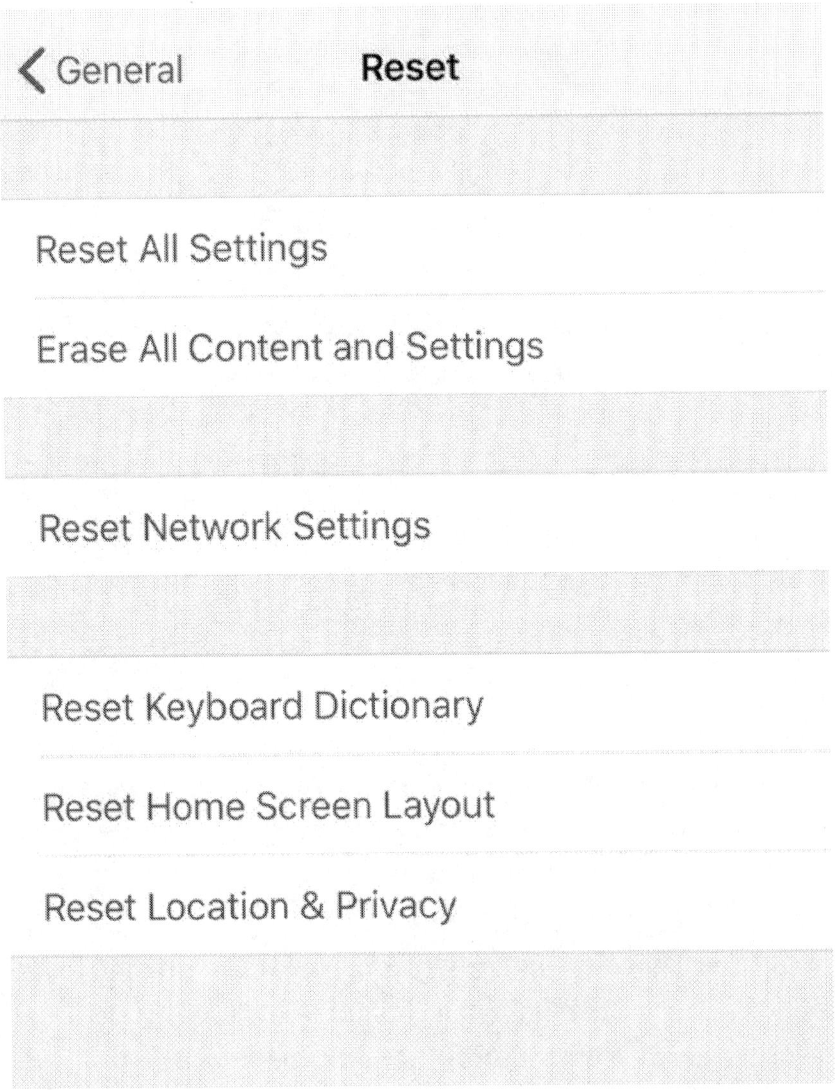

‹ General **Reset**

Reset All Settings

Erase All Content and Settings

Reset Network Settings

Reset Keyboard Dictionary

Reset Home Screen Layout

Reset Location & Privacy

iPhone reset options

For starters, if you just want to restart your phone because it's not responding or otherwise acting wonky, here are the ways to do it, according to Apple.

On an iPhone 8 or later: Press and quickly release the Volume Up button. Press and quickly release the Volume Down button. Then press and hold the Side button until you see the Apple logo.

On an iPhone 7 or iPhone 7 Plus: Press and hold both the Side and Volume Down buttons for at least 10 seconds, until you see the Apple logo.

On an iPhone 6s and earlier, iPad, or iPod touch: Press and hold both the Home and the Top (or Side) buttons for at least 10 seconds, until you see the Apple logo.

Now, if you need some more horsepower behind your reset, you'll want to go into Settings > General > Reset to see your options.

Scroll all the way to the bottom to see the Reset section. Under it, you'll see an option to Shut Down your phone as well.

Before we proceed, don't worry, you can tap Reset and you won't do anything harmful to your phone. You will be presented with a very clear menu before you actually apply any changes.

Now, let's go through your options.

Reset All Settings

"This will reset all settings and your Apple Pay cards will be removed. No data or media will be deleted."

Think of this as your first line of defense when something is bugging you about your phone. Maybe it's a ringtone you can't seem to change or some odd thing that keeps happening that never happened in the past. Choosing this option won't delete any data or accounts you've added to your device, but it will put all settings back to their factory defaults including your ringtones, display settings, network settings and basically anything else you're customized on your phone.

I would do this when your phone keeps crashing or an app keeps hanging or you are about to pull your hair out because something changed and messed things up but you can't figure out what it is. It will take you some time to get your phone back up to speed with all of your preferences.

Erase All Content and Settings

"This will delete all media and data, and reset all settings."

You shouldn't really need this option unless you are selling your iPhone or trading it back in. Choosing this option will literally wipe your phone clean of everything you've put on there including photos, data and anything that wasn't there when the phone was first taken out of the box.

When you choose this option, iCloud should prompt you to complete a backup of your device. Yes, you should complete a backup of your device before you do this since all of your photos and data will be destroyed in the process. If it's up in iCloud, you'll be able to re-download it to your new device. If you skip this backup, you better know what you're doing.

If you are selling your phone or giving it to a friend, definitely use the Erase All Content and Settings option before you hand your device over. This process should also log you out of iCloud, which means it will be easier for your friend or buyer to set up your phone new. Just keep in mind if you Erase All Content and Settings, someone with access to your phone could set it up as theirs since it's no longer protected by a passcode or Face ID.

Reset Network Settings

This will delete all network settings, returning them to factory defaults.

You can use this option if you're having some sort of connectivity issue with Bluetooth, WiFi or Cellular Data. If you choose to do this, all of your saved WiFi networks will be cleared out, as well as any devices you've paired with your phone via Bluetooth.

You can also try this option if you are having trouble with Visual Voicemail.

Reset Keyboard Dictionary

This will delete all custom words you have typed on the keyboard, returning the keyboard dictionary to factory defaults.

Since the iOS keyboard learns how you type, you might notice some suggestions and corrections that throw you for a loop. While there are ways to manually delete these, there might be a time when you just want to start fresh. This option will accomplish that.

Reset Home Screen Layout

This will reset your home screen layout to factory defaults.

If you're like many iPhone users, you've probably spent a fair amount of time arranging the icons on your home screen. This will make all of your efforts null and void in about a second or two.

Select this option and all of your icons will jump into the places they were when you originally took your iPhone out of the box. This means Mail will sit in the upper left-hand corner of your home screen, followed by Calendar, Photos, Camera, Maps, Clock, News, etc. In your dock will be the Phone, Safari, Messages and Music.

What about the rest of your icons? They'll appear on the second screen, after some additional Apple system icons like FaceTime, Calculator and Watch. But the neat thing is that all of the apps you installed will be in alphabetical order. So if you're a total neat freak, it wouldn't take you much longer to put the Apple system icons where they fall in the alphabetical order too.

To some, the Reset Home Screen Layout will be a well-needed adjustment, to others, it might be the worst possible thing that could happen to their carefully curated home screen.

Reset Location & Privacy

This will reset your location and privacy settings to factory defaults.

With everything happening with Privacy these days, this setting can be a handy one. It will sort of give you all of your privacy back since it resets all requests to use items like your Location, Contacts, Calendar, Photos, Microphone camera and more.

Also, all apps will be stripped of their permission to access anything on your phone in the Privacy section like the items I just mentioned. For this reason, choosing to reset these settings can be a blessing or a curse. If you're worried that you changed something in the past when it comes to your privacy, resetting here can bring the thing back to the way your phone was when it arrived. You'll just have to re-authorize apps as you open them. For instance, if Instagram was previously able to access your camera to help you post a Story, the next time you go to post a Story the app will have to re-request access to your camera and perhaps the microphone and your location.

About the Author

Rich DeMuro is the tech reporter for KTLA-TV Channel 5 in Los Angeles and appears on the #1 rated KTLA Morning News. Viewers around the nation know him as "Rich on Tech" and his syndicated segment runs on dozens of TV stations.

Rich regularly appears on KFI AM 640 Los Angeles, TWiT and The Tech Guy Radio show. He has appeared on NBC's Today Show, ABC News, Fox News Channel, the BBC, Entertainment Tonight, Home & Family, G4TV, CNBC and more.

Rich is originally from New Jersey and resides in Los Angeles with his wife and two sons.

Contact Rich:

RichOnTech.tv

@richdemuro on Twitter

@richontech on Instagram

facebook.com/richontech

#101HandyTechTips